For the afghan you see here,
thanks to Cascade Yarns for the beautiful wools;
thanks to our knitters: Karen Bright, Anne Claxon,
Joni Coniglio, Jennifer Dyke, Mary Lou Eastman,
Angela Gier, Rick Mondragon, Sue Kay Nelson,
Elaine Rowley, Natalie Sorenson, Carol Thompson,
Lizbeth Upitis;
and thanks to Artisan House Galleries in Sioux
Falls for the use of their showroom and Stickley
collections (see pages 1 and 2–3).

STICKLEY MISSION CLASSICS COLLECTION, PRAIRIE PANEL SETTLE AND WOOD TOP COCKTAIL TABLE

STICKLEY METROPOLITAN COLLECTION, LINGERIE CHEST

Since its first appearance in Knitter's Magazine issues 42–46, the Great American Afghan has appealed to many knitters—especially first-time afghan knitters, even those who thought they would never knit an afghan.

The secret of its success is the square. You'll explore a broad range of knitting techniques, one square at a time.

You'll encounter entrelac. Try Barbara Venishnick's Square 19; you'll see how that distinctive interlaced pattern builds. Then on to Betty Anne Lampers' Square 12 for an entrelac stitch sampler. For more adventure, try Karen Kendrick-Hands' Square 17, where entrelac worked in the round becomes truly sculptural. Knitting just these three squares will transform the way you look a pair of needles and a ball of yarn.

Since the squares are made one at a time, they are portable and interchangeable. You're free: choose a square or a color to repeat or omit, developing your ideas as you go.

TONAL...

Here 4 colors of Cascade 220 Wool (2435, 9463, 7829, 2451) are worked with 2 colors of Madil Kid Seta (681 and 682) to produce 8 blends and a wonderfully luxurious fabric.

ANALAGOUS...

In Pastaza a llama/ wool blend, colors 271, 070, 045, 079, 272, 1010, 052, 028, and 067: since this yarn is a bit heavier, we used 1 size larger needle for 13″ squares.

OR WILD

In Dolce, a blend of alpaca, wool, and silk, colors 965, 927, 956, 973, 913, 943, 934, 955, 953, 963, 926 gave us a playful palette.

All yarns by Cascade Yarns.

Visit **www.knittinguniverse.com** to color and assemble your own afghan with **Knitter's Paintbox**.

1 2 3 **4** 5 6

CASCADE 220 wool; 3.5oz (100g); 220yds (200m)

Skeins of yarn and approximate yardage required to
work the afghan as pictured.

#2440	four	675 yds
#2452	three	450 yds
#9489	three	470 yds
#9445	two	390 yds
* #2444	one	30 yds
#2435	two	355 yds
#2445	two	251 yds
#9408	one	90 yds
#2453	three	592 yds
#9488	one	110 yds

* Optional, used in Square 1 only.

Knitting Notes

1 Don't think of all of these squares as equals. Some are fairly simple, others a bit more challenging.

2 You don't need to make an exact copy of our afghan. Arrange the squares any way you like. You may choose to repeat several of your favorite squares, or build your afghan with just one pattern.

3 Adjust the number of squares to suit your project; fewer squares make a crib blanket, more make a bedspread.

4 Due to the nature of the various patterns, all squares may not block to an exact 12" square. When sewn together, small differences in size will ease into shape.

5 The needle sizes suggested for the individual squares vary, depending on the stitch patterns. As always, the sizes listed are merely a starting point; choose the needle size that gives you the correct gauge.

6 Our edging was intended to frame the afghan without detracting from its amazing content. You may prefer to work around the piece in single crochet in one color and then work another row in a second color in reverse single crochet. Use two strands of yarn and a size H or I (5.00 or 5.50mm) hook.

Visit **www.knittinguniverse.com** to color and assemble your own afghan with **Knitter's Paintbox**.

AFGHAN FINISHED MEASUREMENTS
62" x 62"

1	2	3	4	5
6	7	8	9	10
11	12	13	14	15
16	17	18	19	20
21	22	23	24	25

EACH SQUARE MEASUREMENTS
Approximately 12" x 12"

5 easiest squares:
3 Traci Bunkers
8 Kathy Zimmerman
13 Nicky Epstein
14 Sidna Farley
22 Heather Lodinsky

5 most challenging squares:
7 Susan Z. Douglas
12 Bette Anne Lampers
16 Julie Hoff-Weisenberger
17 Karen Kendrick-Hands
21 Sally Melville

Finishing The Afghan

Pin square to 12" and steam; never place the iron directly onto your knit piece.

Sew squares together using grid shown above, fudging a bit if necessary. Use a strand of the most prominent color of the two squares you are joining. We found it most successful to seam from right side (as shown below).

Edging

Note Use any 2 colors desired. We used #9489 (burgundy) and #9488 (red).
With right side of afghan facing, size 9 (5.5mm) circular needle, 2 strands of burgundy, and beginning 1 square in from a corner, pick up and knit approximately 40–46 stitches along first square. Do not turn work. *Slide stitches to other end of the needle and attach 2 strands of red. Working with red only, bind off in purl until 1 stitch remains. Leave stitch live and don't cut yarn. Using burgundy, pick up along next square. Rep from* around entire afghan omitting yarn attachment. Fasten off last stitch and join beginning to end. Weave in ends.

SEAMING GARTER EDGES

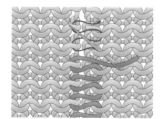

1 Place pieces side by side, with right sides facing you.
2 Thread blunt needle with yarn to match piece.
3 Pick up or catch a lower garter ridge from one piece (right piece, above).
4 Cross to matching place on other piece and pick up or catch an upper garter ridge (left piece, above).
5 Repeat Steps 3 & 4, pulling thread taut as you go.

SEAMING CAST-ON TO BIND-OFF

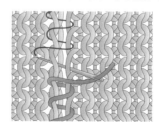

1 Place pieces side by side, with right sides facing you.
2 Thread blunt needle with yarn to match piece.
3 Pick up or catch a front leg of cast-on (right piece, above).
4 Cross to matching place on other piece and pick up or catch a front loop on bind-off (left piece, above).
5 Repeat Steps 3 & 4 pulling thread taut as you go.

Priscilla Gibson-Roberts
CEDAREDGE, COLORADO

Since my mother did not knit, I cannot claim that I have been knitting forever—besides, growing up in South Texas one has little need for warm woolies! At graduate school way up North, I was exposed to a colder climate and a dorm mate with knitting expertise.

In working on my book, Ethnic Socks & Stockings, I discovered nirvana. In a former life, I must have been a nomad, roaming the steppes and deserts behind my flock while spinning and knitting exquisite socks! The design of my block expresses my love of both the Eastern designs and the techniques found in these socks!

Yarn colors
MC #2440
A #9489
B #2444

10cm/4"

32

22
• *over stockinette stitch (k on RS, p on WS), using larger needles*

• 3.75mm/US 5 and 4mm/US6, or size to obtain gauge, 60cm/24" long

• Five 2mm/US 0

&

• cable needle (cn)
• stitch markers
• yarn needle
• small tapestry needle for grafting

This square originally appeared in Knitter's K44.

Note
See *School*, page 60, for SSK, invisible cast-on, straight-wrap cast-on, grafting, Make 1 knit (M1K), Make 1 purl (M1P), knit into front and back of st (kf&b), duplicate st, tassels, and twisted cord.

Square
With smaller circular needle and MC, using invisible cast-on, cast on 40 sts.
Row 1 (RS) P17, k23.
Row 2 P23, k17.
Row 3 Repeat row 1.
Beg Heart Chart Cont to work St st over 23 sts and work Heart Chart over 17 sts until 16 rows of Heart Chart have been worked 3 times.
Next row (WS) P23, k17.
Next row P17, k23.
With RS facing, place marker (pm), pick up and k 40 sts along edge of square to cast-on edge, pm, place 40 sts from cast-on onto left needle, removing waste yarn and knit across, pm, pick up and k 40 sts along edge of square, pm for beg of rnd—160 sts. Join and knit 1 rnd.
Next rnd [Kf&b, k to 1 st before marker, kf&b, slip marker] 4 times—168 sts. Rep last 2 rnds 7 times more—224 sts. Change to larger needle. [P 1 rnd, k 1 rnd working incs as before] twice—240 sts.
Next rnd Purl. Bind off.

Finishing
With A, work vertical row of Double knot st between panels of St st/rev St st, then work row around outside edge of rev St st and St st square. With A, work Duplicate St Chart as shown in photo, then with B, work chart on the other sides.

Miniature socks (*MAKE 2*)
(**Note** Socks are knit with 2 plies of the 4-ply yarn. To divide yarn, spread plies at end, grasp 2 and draw out while sliding down rem 2 plies. Divide 12 yds of A and 6 yds of B.)
With dpns and A, cast on 5 sts using straight-wrap cast-on. There are 5 loops on the top needle and 5 on the bottom.

Next rnd Needle 1, pick up and k 1 st along edge of piece, k3; needle 2, k2, pick up and k 1 st along edge of piece; needle 3, pick up and k 1 st along edge of piece, k2; needle 4, k3, pick up and k 1 st along edge of piece—14 sts, arranged on needles: 4-3-3-4.
Next (Inc) rnd [K1, M1K, k to end of needle, k to st before end of needle, M1K, k1] twice.
Next rnd Knit.
Rep last 2 rnds once, then Inc rnd once more—26 sts, 7-6-6-7.
Work Foot and Leg Chart rnds 1–14.
Mark for heel With waste yarn, k13 (across needles 1 and 2).
Leg With A, beg with needle 1 (where yarn is waiting) work chart rnd 15. Work Foot and Leg chart rnds 16–37. Bind off as you work chart rnd 38.
Heel Remove waste yarn, placing 13 sts each on 2 dpns—26 sts. **Rnd 1** With A and needle 1, k13; needle 2, k7; needle 3, k6. Work Heel Chart rnds 2–8. Slip sts from needle 3 onto needle 2—5 sts on each needle. Graft sts.
Twisted cords Cut two 30" lengths each of A and B. Make 2 cords with 1 length of each color.
Tassels Make a tassel and attach to tied end of each cord. Following photo, attach socks, cords and tassels to square.

IN OTHER WORDS
1/1 RPC Sl 1 to cn, hold to back, k1; p1 from cn
1/1 LPC Sl 1 to cn, hold to front, p1; k1 from cn
L dec K1, sl 1, pass k st over sl st
R dec Sl 1, k1, sl both sts to left needle, pass k st over sl st, sl the sl st to right needle
Heart Chart
Row 1 (WS) K8, p1, k8. *2* P8, M1K, k1, M1K, p8. *3* K6, SSK, p3, k2tog, k6. *4* P7, k1, M1K, k1, M1K, k1, p7. *5* K5, SSK, p5, k2tog, k5. *6* P6, k2, M1K, k1, M1K, k2, p6. *7* K4, SSK, p7, k2tog, k4. *8* P5, k3, M1K, k1, M1K, k3, p5. *9* K3, SSK, p9, k2tog, k3. *10* P4, k4, M1K, k1, M1K, k4, p4. *11* K2, SSK, p5, k1, p5, k2tog, k2. *12* P3, 1/1LPC, k1, 1/1RPC, p1, 1/1LPC, k1, 1/1RPC, p3. *13* K4, 1/1RPC, p1, k3, p1, 1/1LPC, k4. *14* P4, L dec, p2, M1P, p1, M1P, p2, R dec, p4. *15* Knit. *16* Purl.

Duplicate St Chart

Center

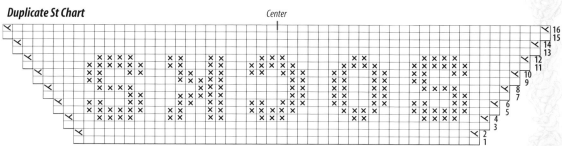

40-st to 56-st repeat

Foot & Leg Chart

38

30

20

15 — Mark for heel
14

10

1

13-st repeat

Heart Chart

16
15
14
13
12
11
10
9
8
7
6
5
4
3
2
1

17 sts

	K on RS, p on WS
	P on RS, k on WS
	K2tog on WS
	SSK on WS
	M1K, k1, M1K
	K in front & back of st (kf&b)
	M1P, p1, M1P
	1/1 RPC
	1/1 LPC
	L dec
	R dec
	Duplicate st

DOUBLE KNOT ST

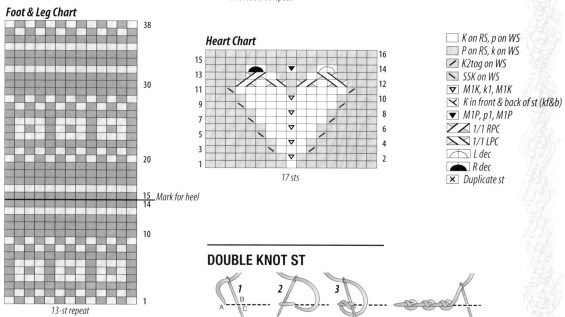

Only in step 1 does needle go through fabric.
In steps 2 and 3 needle goes under AB stitch to form knot.

Heel Chart

8

5

1

13-st to 5-st repeat

	A
	B

Paula B. Levy
EAST WINDSOR, NEW JERSEY

I learned to knit as an adult when I was inspired by the beautiful sweaters in a magazine. My first project was a self-designed vest. I haven't looked back.

I began experimenting with construction methods. Add to this my degree in mathematics, and it's no surprise that my work tends to be very geometric. I decided to make my square a shape within a shape within a shape and so on. One of my favorite techniques is outlining shapes with one-over-one cable twists.

Yarn color #2445

10cm/4"

24

17

• **over stockinette stitch**
(k on RS, p on WS)

• 5mm/US 8

&

• cable needle (cn)

This square originally appeared in Knitter's K45.

Notes
1 To create horizontal lines of inner rev St st square, bind off on 1 row and, on next row, pick up sts in purl bumps immediately under bound-off sts. The first 16 purl bumps will be obvious. For 17th st, pick st up wherever it looks best from RS. **2** To perfect corners of inner rev St st square, bind off final st directly tog with foll st. In one case, this also involves a cable twist—explained in instructions.

Square
Cast on 56 sts. K 5 rows, dec 5 sts on last (WS) row—51 sts. **Beg Chart: Row 1** (RS) K3, work chart pat over 45 sts, k3. Keeping first and last 3 sts in garter st, work chart over 45 center sts through chart row 62, k 1 row, inc 5 sts—56 sts. K 5 rows. Bind off.

Finishing
When pinning out to block, also pin inner shapes so that sides of inner square are straight and sides of diamonds curve in.

IN OTHER WORDS
RC (On RS rows) Sl 1 to cn, hold in back, k1; k1 from cn. (WS rows) Sl 1 to cn, hold in back, p1; p1 from cn.
LC (On RS rows) Sl 1 to cn, hold in front, k1; k1 from cn. (WS rows) Sl 1 to cn, hold in front, p1; p1 from cn.
RPC Sl 1 to cn, hold in back, k1; p1 from cn.
LPC Sl 1 to cn, hold in front, p1; k1 from cn.

Special instructions
Row 19 Sl 1 to cn, hold to front, return last st on right needle to left needle and k2tog (returned st with st next to it), k1 from cn.
Row 20 Pick up 7 sts knitwise by inserting right needle from bottom to top under purl bump, wrap yarn and knit up loop. Pick up 3 sts purlwise as foll: with yarn in front, insert right needle from top to bottom under purl bump and purl up loop. Pick up 7 sts knitwise. See Note 1 for 17th st. *Row 44* Sl next st knitwise, return it (in twisted position) and previous st on right needle to left needle and p2tog tbl.
Row 45 (RS) The purl bumps will be behind bound-off sts. With yarn in back, put needle under purl bump from top to bottom and k up a st. See Note 1 for 17th st.

Chart Pat *OVER 45 STS*
Row 1 (RS) K45. *2* K21, p3, k21. *3* P20, RC, k1, LC, p20. *4* K20, p5, k20. *5* P19, RC, k3, LC, p19. *6* K19, p7, k19. *7* P18, RC, k5, LC, p18. *8* K18, p9, k18. *9* P17, RC, k7, LC, p17. *10* K17, p11, k17. *11* P16, RC, k9, LC, p16. *12* K16, p13, k16. *13* P15, RC, k11, LC, p15. *14* K15, p15, k15. *15* P14, RC, k13, LC, p14. *16* K14, p17, k14. *17* P13, RC, k15, LC, p13. *18* K13, p19, k13. *19* P12, RC, Bind off 16, foll special instructions, p12. *20* K11, LC, p1, foll special instructions, p1, RC, k11. *21* P10, RC, k2, p7, k3, p7, k2, LC, p10. *22* K9, LC, p3, k6, LC, p1, RC, k6, p3, RC, k9. *23* P8, RC, k4, p6, k5, p6, k4, LC, p8. *24* K7, LC, p5, k5, LC, p3, RC, k5, p5, RC, k7. *25* P6, RC, k6, p5, k7, p5, k6, LC, p6. *26* K5, LC, p7, k4, LC, p5, RC, k4, p7, RC, k5. *27* P4, RC, k8, p4, k9, p4, k8, LC, p4. *28* K3, LC, p9, k3, LC, p7, RC, k3, p9, RC, k3. *29* P2, RC, k10, p2, RC, k9, LC, p2, k10, LC, p2. *30* K1, LC, p11, k1, LC, p11, RC, k1, p11, RC, k1. *31* RC, k12, RC, k13, LC, k12, LC. *32* Purl. *33* LPC, k12, LPC, k13, RPC, k12, RPC. *34* K1, RPC, p11, k1, RPC, p11, LPC, k1, p11, LPC, k1. *35* P2, LPC, k10, p2, LPC, k9, RPC, p2, k10, RPC, p2. *36* K3, RPC, p9, k3, RPC, p7, LPC, k3, p9, LPC, k3. *37* P4, LPC, k8, p4, k9, p4, k8, RPC, p4. *38* K5, RPC, p7, k4, RPC, p5, LPC, k4, p7, LPC, k5. *39* P6, LPC, k6, p5, k7, p5, k6, RPC, p6. *40* K7, RPC, p5, k5, RPC, p3, LPC, k5, p5, LPC, k7. *41* P8, LPC, k4, p6, k5, p6, k4, RPC, p8. *42* K9, RPC, p3, k6, RPC, p1, LPC, k6, p3, LPC, k9. *43* P10, LPC, k2, p7, k3, p7, k2, RPC, p10. *44* K11, RPC, p1, bind off 16 in purl, foll special instructions, LPC, k11. *45* P12, LPC, pick up 17 sts in purl bumps of bound-off sts, foll special instructions, RPC, p12. *46* K13, p19, k13. *47* P13, LPC, k15, RPC, p13. *48* K14, p17, k14. *49* P14, LPC, k13, RPC, p14. *50* K15, p15, k15. *51* P15, LPC, k11, RPC, p15. *52* K16, p13, k16. *53* P16, LPC, k9, RPC, p16. *54* K17, p11, k17. *55* P17, LPC, k7, RPC, p17. *56* K18, p9, k18. *57* P18, LPC, k5, RPC, p18. *58* K19, p7, k19. *59* P19, LPC, k3, RPC, p19. *60* K20, p5, k20. *61* P20, LPC, k1, RPC, p20. *62* K21, p3, k21.

□ K on RS, p on WS
▨ P on RS, k on WS
▨ RC
▧ LC
▨ RPC
▧ LPC
⌢ BO on RS in k, on WS in p
✳ See Special Instructions
● See Special Instructions

Chart Pat

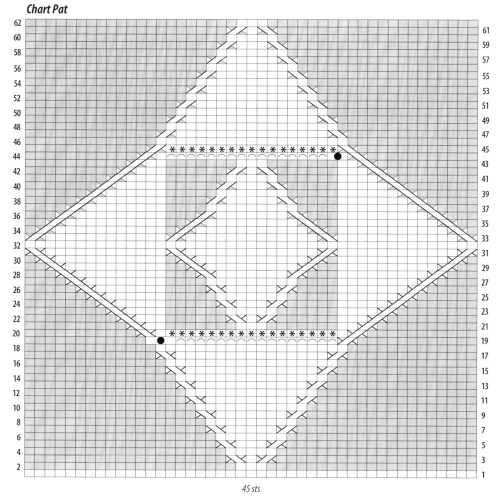

45 sts

Traci Bunkers
LAWRENCE, KANSAS

I learned to knit in college, and I immediately started designing my own sweaters instead of using patterns.

I feel it is important not only for my designs to be attractive but also to feel good. I choose the fibers and design the stitch patterns accordingly. I want the experience to be both visual and tactile. This square shows my love for textures: cables, bobbles, and knit/purl combinations all in one square. It's so exciting when all of the pieces come together. I like the challenge of designing something that looks complicated, but isn't. I create stitch patterns that use the same number of row repeats and are easy to memorize.

Yarn color #2453

10cm/4"

28

20

• over stockinette stitch
(k on RS, p on WS)

• 4.5mm/US 7

&

• cable needle (cn)

This square originally appeared in Knitter's K46.

Note
See *School*, page 60, for SSK and yo before a k and p st.

Square
Cast on 59 sts. K 5 rows. **Beg Chart Pat: Row 1** (RS) K3, work Chart Pat over 53 sts, k3. Keeping first and last 3 sts in garter st, cont in chart pat over center 53 sts until piece measures approx 11¼" from beg, end with chart row 8. K 6 rows. Bind off.

IN OTHER WORDS
1/1 RC Sl 1 to cn and hold to back, k1; k1 from cn.
1/1 LC Sl 1 to cn and hold to front, k1; k1 from cn.
3/3 RC Sl 3 to cn, hold to back, k3; k3 from cn.
3/3 LC Sl 3 to cn, hold to front, k3; k3 from cn.
Make bobble (MB) [K1, yo, k1, yo, k1] all in one st, turn. P5, turn. K5, turn. P2tog, p1, p2tog, turn. K3tog—1 st.

Chart Pat *OVER 53 STS*
Row 1 (RS) P1, yo, k2, k2tog, k6, SSK, k2, yo, p1, [p1, k1] 3 times, p2, k2, p1, k2, p1, [p1, k1] 3 times, p2, yo, k2, k2tog, k6, SSK, k2, yo, p1. *2 and all WS rows* K the knit sts and bobbles, and p the purl sts and yo's. *3* P1, yo, k2, k2tog, k6, SSK, k2, yo, p9, k2, p1, k2, p9, yo, k2, k2tog, k6, SSK, k2, yo, p1. *5* P1, yo, k2, k2tog, 3/3 RC, SSK, k2, yo, p1, [p1, k1] 3 times, p2, 1/1 RC, MB, 1/1 LC, p1, [p1, k1] 3 times, p2, yo, k2, k2tog, 3/3 LC, SSK, k2, yo, p1. *7* Rep row 3. *9* Rep row 1. *11* P1, yo, k2, k2tog, k6, SSK, k2, yo, p9, 1/1 RC, p1, 1/1 LC, p9, yo, k2, k2tog, k6, SSK, k2, yo, p1. *12* Rep row 2. Rep rows 1–12 for Chart Pat.

K on RS, p on WS
P on RS, k on WS
⊙ Yarn over (yo)
✓ K2tog
✓ SSK
B Make bobble (MB)
1/1 RC
1/1 LC
3/3 RC
3/3 LC

Chart Pat

53 sts

Celeste Pinheiro
BEAVERTON, OREGON

My inspiration for this square came from my childhood. I grew up surrounded by nature, and it continues to inspire me in my knitting in both color and texture.

I explored knitting's sculptural side with Aran stitches, I-cord, and shaping in this square. I always enjoy coming up with something different, fun, and even a little wild.

Yarn color #2452

10cm/4"

32

18
**· over Seed St,
using larger needles**

· 4mm/US 6 and 4.5mm/US 7, or size to obtain gauge

· two 4mm/US 6

&

· cable needle (cn)

This square originally appeared in Knitter's K46.

Notes
1 See *School,* page 60, for SSK, I-cord, and wrapping sts on short rows. *2* Refer to square 6, pg 18, for French knot embroidery.

Seed St
Row 1 *K1, p1; rep from *. *2* K the purl sts and p the knit sts. Rep row 2 for seed st.

Square
With smaller needles, cast on 60 sts. K 5 rows. Change to larger needles. *Next row* (RS) K26, inc 4 sts evenly across (to 30), k to end—64 sts. *Preparation row* (WS) K3, [p1, k1] 14 times, k4, p3, k2, p3, k6, p3, k2, p3, k7. *Beg Wave Pat Chart and Seed St: Row 1* (RS) K3, work Wave Pat Chart over 30 sts, work Seed St over 28 sts, k3. *Row 2* K3, work Seed St over 28 sts, work Wave Pat Chart over 30 sts, k3. Cont in pats as established, AT SAME TIME, when piece measures approx 1", 6", and 11", work 2 short rows in Seed St portion as foll: on a WS row, k3, work 28 sts in Seed St, wrap next st and turn, work to end of next (RS) row. Cont working over all sts until next pair of short rows. When piece measures 11½" from beg, end with a WS row. Change to smaller needles. *Next row* (RS) K30, dec 4 sts evenly across (to 26), k to end—60 sts. K 5 rows. Bind off.

Appliques
(*Note* Work all appliques with smaller needles.)
Fish *MAKE 3*
Cast on 11 sts. Work rows 1–22 of Fish Chart. Fasten off. Embroider French knot eye. Wrap tail as shown in diagram. Using photo as guide, sew fish in place.
Crab
Legs With dpns, work six 4-st I-cords as foll: make 2 cords each 1" long (claw bases), 2 each 2½" long (lower legs), and 2 each 4½" long (upper legs).
Left Claw Cast on 6 sts. Work rows 1–4 of Left Claw Chart. *Row 5* (WS) P7 (for first section), turn, leaving rem 7 sts on hold for 2nd section. Work first section through chart row 14. Fasten off. With WS facing, rejoin yarn for 2nd section and work chart rows 5–10.
Right Claw Work as for left claw, reversing placement of sections.
Body Cast on 11 sts. Work rows 1–15 of Crab Body Chart. Bind off 17 sts. Embroider French knot eyes. Using photo as guide, sew pieces in place, folding legs in half.
Shell
With dpns, cast on 4 sts. Work I-cord for 9". Beg working back and forth in St st, inc 1 st at end of every knit row 5 times—9 sts. Bind off. Coil I-cord (as shown) and sew in place, letting flat portion puff up a little.

IN OTHER WORDS
3/2 RPC Sl 2 to cn, hold to back, k3; p2 from cn.
3/2 LPC Sl 3 to cn, hold to front, p2; k3 from cn.

Wave Pat Chart *OVER 30 STS*
Row 1 (RS) P1, [p3, k3, p2, k3, p3] twice, p1. *2 and all WS rows* K the knit sts and p the purl sts. *3* P1, [p1, 3/2 RPC, p2, 3/2 LPC, p1] twice, p1. *5* P1, [P1, k3, p6, k3, p1] twice, p1. *7* P1, [p1, 3/2 LPC, p2, 3/2 RPC, p1] twice, p1. *8* Rep row 2. Rep rows 1–8 for Wave Pat Chart.

Fish Chart *BEGIN ON 11 STS*
Rows 1 and 3 (WS) [P1, k1] 5 times, p1. *2 and 4* [K1, p1] 5 times, k1. *5* P1, [p3tog] 3 times, p1—5 sts. *6* K2, yo, k1, yo, k2—7 sts. *7 and all foll WS rows* Purl. *8* K3, yo, k1, yo, k3—9 sts. *10* K4, yo, k1, yo, k4—11 sts. *12* K11. *14, 16, 18 and 20* SSK, k to last 2 sts, k2tog. *22* K3tog—1 st.

Crab Left Claw Chart *BEGIN ON 6 STS*
Row 1 and all WS rows Purl. *2* [K1, yo] twice, k2, [yo, k1] twice—10 sts. *4* K2, yo, k1, yo, k4, yo, k1, yo, k2—14 sts. *First section: Row 5* P7, turn. *6* K3, yo, k1, yo, k3. *8, 10 and 12* SSK, k to last 2 sts, k2tog. *14* K3tog—1 st. *Second section: Row 5* (WS) P7. *6 and 8* SSK, k to last 2 sts, k2tog. *10* K3tog—1 st.

Crab Right Claw Chart *BEGIN ON 6 STS*
Work as for left claw, reversing placement of sections.

Crab Body Chart *BEGIN ON 11 STS*
Row 1 and all WS rows K1, p to last st, k1. *2* K5, yo, k1, yo, k5—13 sts. *4, 8, 12 and 14* Knit. *6* K6, yo, k1, yo, k6—15 sts. *10* K7, yo, k1, yo, k7—17 sts. *15* Rep row 1.

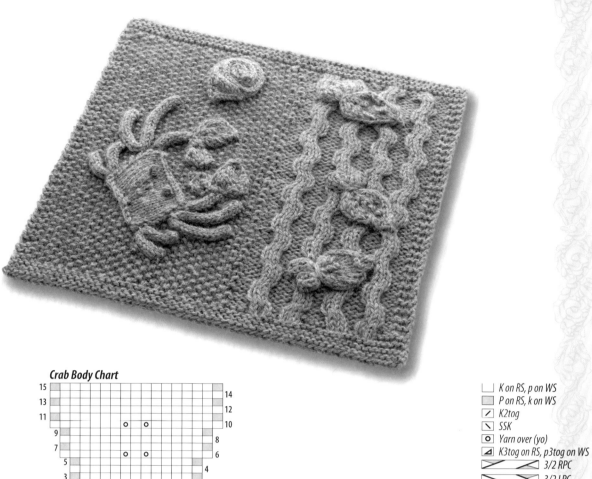

Crab Body Chart

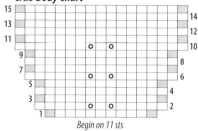

Begin on 11 sts

	K on RS, p on WS
▨	P on RS, k on WS
╱	K2tog
╲	SSK
◯	Yarn over (yo)
◤	K3tog on RS, p3tog on WS
▱	3/2 RPC
▱	3/2 LPC

Wave Pat Chart

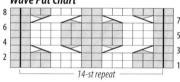

14-st repeat

Fish Chart

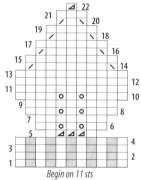

Begin on 11 sts

Crab Left Claw Chart

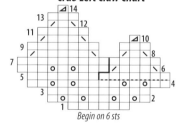

Begin on 6 sts

Fish

wrap a few times
to pull in this way

wrap tight a few times
to pull in this way

Shell

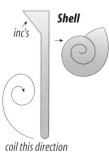

inc's

coil this direction

Crab Right Claw Chart

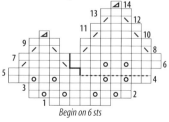

Begin on 6 sts

Note for claw charts:

Work each section above row 4 (shown divided by dark line) separately.

Jacqueline Jewett
BLAUVELT, NEW YORK

I came to the United States from London in the '70s to pursue a career in advertising. Through my work, I have had a chance to travel. I instructed crocheters in Barbados and taught sweater and sock making in Kabul, Afghanistan.

I designed the Fanfare stitch pattern for a sweater for Knitter's [K35]. Here the motifs are placed back-to-back on each of the four sections of the square, to form a Victorian-looking floral pattern, with an added leaf in each corner. Further bands of bobbles and eyelet stitches form the border. It is worked with either two straight needles or one circular needle (working back and forth), then joined with an invisible seam along a diagonal.

Yarn color #9445

10cm/4"

28

19
• **over stockinette stitch**
(k on RS, p on WS)

• 4.5mm/US 7, or size to obtain gauge • One 2.75mm/US 2 for cast-on

This square originally appeared in Knitter's K46.

Note
See *School*, page 60, for SSK and SK2P.

Square
With smaller needle, cast on 5 sts. Change to larger needles. Work rows 1–42 of Chart Pat—169 sts.
Row 43 (RS) [K1, yo, (k2tog, yo) 10 times, k1, (yo, SSK) 10 times, yo] 4 times, k1—177 sts.
Rows 44, 46, and 48 Knit.
Row 45 [K1, yo, k43, yo] 4 times, k1—185 sts.
Row 47 [K1, yo, k45, yo] 4 times, k1—193 sts.
Row 49 [K1, yo, k47, yo] 4 times, k1—201 sts.
Bind off knitwise. Sew diagonal seam.

IN OTHER WORDS
Make bobble (MB) K into front, back, and front of st, turn. P3, turn. K3, turn. P3, turn. SK2P, k into horizontal thread at base of bobble, and pass 2nd st on right needle over first st.
1/1 RPT K 2nd st in front of first

st, do not sl st off needle; p first st, then sl both sts off needle.
1/1 LPT P 2nd st through back loop behind first st, do not sl st off needle; k first st, then sl both sts off needle.
Chart Pat
Row 1 (RS) [K1, yo] 4 times, k1—9 sts. **2 and 4** Knit. **3** [K1, yo] 8 times, k1—17 sts. **5** K1, [yo, MB,

p1, MB, yo, k1] 4 times—25 sts. **6** K2, [p1, k1, p1, k3] 3 times, p1, k1, p1, k2. **7** [K1, yo, k2, p1, k2, yo] 4 times, k1—33 sts. **8** [K2, (p2, k1) twice] 4 times, k1. **9** K1, [yo, k2tog, yo, k1, p1, k1, yo, SSK, yo, k1] 4 times—41 sts. **10** [K2, (p3, k1) twice] 4 times, k1. **11** [K1, yo, k2tog, yo, k2, p1, k2, yo, SSK, yo] 4 times, k1—49 sts. **12** [K2, (p4, k1) twice] 4 times, k1. **13** [K1, (yo, k2tog) twice, yo, k1, p1, k1, (yo, SSK) twice, yo] 4 times, k1—57 sts. **14** [K2, (p5, k1) twice] 4 times, k1. **15** [K1, (yo, k2tog) twice, yo, k2, p1, k2, (yo, SSK) twice, yo] 4 times, k1—65 sts. **16** [K2, (p6, k1) twice] 4 times, k1. **17** [K1, (yo, k2tog) 3 times, yo, k1, p1, k1, (yo, SSK) 3 times, yo] 4 times, k1—73 sts. **18** [K2, (p7, k1) twice] 4 times, k1. **19** [K1, (yo, k2tog) 3 times, yo, k2, p1, k2, (yo, SSK) 3 times, yo] 4 times, k1—81 sts. **20** [K2, (p8, k1) twice] 4 times, k1. **21** [K1, yo, p1, MB, (k2tog, yo) 3 times, k1, p1, k1, (yo, SSK) 3 times, MB, p1, yo] 4 times, k1—89 sts. **22** [K4, p7, k1, p7, k3] 4 times, k1. **23** [K1, yo, p4, (k2tog, yo) twice, k2, p1, k2, (yo, SSK) twice, p4, yo] 4 times, k1—97 sts. **24** [K6, p6, k1, p6, k5] 4 times, k1. **25** [K1, yo, k1, p4, MB, (k2tog, yo) twice, k1, p1, k1, (yo, SSK) twice, MB, p4, k1, yo] 4 times, k1—105 sts. **26** [K2, p1, k5, p5, k1, p5, k5, p1, k1] 4 times, k1. **27** [K1, yo, k2, p6, k2tog, yo, k2, p1, k2, yo, SSK, p6, k2, yo] 4 times, k1—113 sts. **28** [K2, p2, k6, p4, k1, p4, k6, p2, k1] 4 times, k1. **29** [K1, yo, k3, p6, MB, k2tog, yo, k1, p1, k1, yo, SSK, MB, p6, k3, yo] 4 times, k1—121 sts. **30** [K2, (p3, k7, p3, k1) twice] 4 times, k1. **31** [K1, yo, k4, p8, k2, p1, k2, p8, k4, yo] 4 times, k1—129 sts. **32** [K2, p4, k8, p2, k1, p2, k8, p4, k1] 4 times, k1. **33** [K1, yo, k3, 1/1 RPT, p8, MB, k1, p1, k1, MB, p8, 1/1 LPT, k3, yo] 4 times, k1—137 sts. **34** [K2, p3, k25, p3, k1] 4 times, k1. **35** [K1, yo, k2, 1/1 RPT, p25, 1/1 LPT, k2, yo] 4 times, k1—145 sts. **36** [K2, p2, k29, p2, k1] 4 times, k1. **37** [K1, yo, k1, 1/1 RPT, p29, 1/1 LPT, k1, yo] 4 times, k1—153 sts. **38** [K2, p1, k33, p1, k1] 4 times, k1. **39** [K1, yo, (k2tog, yo) 9 times, k1, (yo, SSK) 9 times, yo] 4 times, k1—161 sts. **40 and 42** Knit. **41** K1, [yo, (p3, MB) 9 times, p3, yo, MB] 4 times—169 sts.

Chart found on pages 32–33

Maureen Egan Emlet
CONCORD, CALIFORNIA

Because I have been knitting since I was five, I am always on the lookout for techniques that are new to me. I don't want to be restricted to any one method—I like them all.

The contrast-color flowers are made of bullion stitches that are embroidered on after the knitting of the square is complete. The flowers in the main color, however, are worked into the knitting—a technique I extrapolated from the cuff of a pair of 19th-century lace knee socks.

Yarn colors
MC #2453
CC #2452

10cm/4"
28
20
• *over stockinette stitch (k on RS, p on WS)*

• 4.5mm/US 7, or size to obtain gauge

&
• cable needle (cn)
• tapestry needle

This square originally appeared in Knitter's K43.

Note
See *School,* page 60, for S2KP2.

Square
With MC, cast on 56 sts. K 5 rows. **Beg Charts A and B: Row 1** (RS) K3, work Chart A over 19 sts, Chart B over 12 sts, Chart A over 19 sts, k3. Keeping first and last 3 sts in garter st, work chart pats as established over center 50 sts until 12 chart rows have been worked 6 times. K 6 rows. Bind off.

Finishing
With CC and tapestry needle, and using photo as guide, embroider a bullion flower in center of each cable of Chart B, then work 1 French knot at center of each flower. Work 3 French knots immediately above center k bullion.

IN OTHER WORDS
K1-long K1, wrapping yarn around needle twice.
Kf-yo-kb K into front of next st leaving on needle, yo, k into back of same st, drop from needle.
K bullion Sl next st onto a cn, wrap yarn 10 times clockwise around stem of st, knit st from cn.
1/1 RC Sl 1 to cn, hold to back, k1; k1 from cn.
1/1 LC Sl 1 to cn, hold to front, k1; k1 from cn.
1/1 RPC Sl 1 to cn, hold to back, k1; p1 from cn.
1/1 LPC Sl 1 to cn, hold to front, p1; k1 from cn.
1/1 RSPC Sl 1 to cn, hold to back, sl 1 (on row 3, drop both wraps of k1-long); p1 from cn.
1/1 LSPC Sl 1 to cn (on row 3, drop both wraps of k1-long), hold to front, p1; sl 1 from cn.

Chart A *OVER 19 STS*
(**Note** Sl sts purlwise with yarn at WS of work.)
Row 1 (RS) 1/1 RC, p15, 1/1 RC. **2** P2, k6, k1-long, k1, k1-long, k6, p2. **3** 1/1 LC, p5, 1/1 RSPC (dropping both wraps of k1-long), k1 tbl, 1/1 LSPC (dropping both wraps of k1-long), p5, 1/1 LC. **4** P2, k5, sl 1, k1, p1, k1, sl 1, k5, p2. **5** 1/1 RC, p4, 1/1 RSPC, p1, k1 tbl, p1, 1/1 LSPC, p4, 1/1 RC. **6** P2, k4, [p1, k2] twice, p1, k4, p2. **7** 1/1 LC, p7, k1 tbl, p7, 1/1 LC. **8** P2, k7, kf-yo-kb, k7, p2—21 sts. **9** 1/1 RC, p7, [k bullion] 3 times, p7, 1/1 RC. **10** P2, k7, sl 3, k7, p2. **11** 1/1 LC, p7, S2KP2, p7, 1/1 LC—19 sts. **12** P2, k15, p2.
Rep rows 1–12 for Chart A.

Chart B *OVER 12 STS*
Row 1 (RS) P5, 1/1 RC, p5. **2 and all WS rows** K the knit sts and p the purl sts. **3** P4, 1/1 RPC, 1/1 LPC, p4. **5** P3, 1/1 RPC, p2, 1/1 LPC, p3. **7** P3, k1, p4, k1, p3. **9** P3, 1/1 LPC, p2, 1/1 RPC, p3. **11** P4, 1/1 LPC, 1/1 RPC, p4. **12** Rep row 2.
Rep rows 1–12 for Chart B.

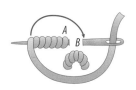

Bullion knot
Work as for French knot, wrapping thread 10 times around needle. For bullion-st flowers, work three bullion sts, overlapping them in a circle. Work a French knot in the center of each flower.

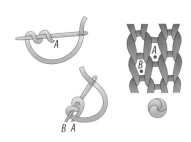

French knot
Bring the needle out where needed. Just above where the yarn comes through the fabric, wind the yarn around the tip of needle twice. Holding the wraps with your thumb, insert the needle back through fabric one thread over from the beginning point.

Chart A

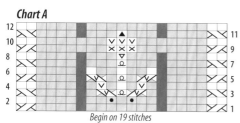

Begin on 19 stitches

Chart B

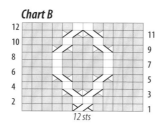

12 sts

☐ K on RS, p on WS
▨ P on RS, k on WS
⟐ K 1 through back loop (tbl)
∨ Slip 1 purlwise with yarn at WS of work
▓ Sts do not exist in these areas of chart
▲ S2KP2
• K1-long
▽ Kf-yo-kb
✕ K bullion
⟋✕ 1/1 RC
✕⟍ 1/1 LC
⟋ 1/1 RPC
⟍ 1/1 LPC
⟋✓ 1/1 RSPC
✓⟍ 1/1 LSPC

Susan Z. Douglas

TOPSHAM, MAINE

I cut my knitting teeth on the craft magazines of the mid-'70s, and needlework publications have been intertwined with my life ever since. When the November 1980 issue of Mon Tricot Knit and Crochet was delivered to my door, I was bowled over by a child's sweater banded with oak leaves and acorns. More than 10 years later, with many knitting tricks up my sleeve and after a few tries, I developed the acorn and leaf that you see here.

Note

See *School*, page 60, for Make 1 purl (M1P), SSP, S2KP2, and wrapping sts on short rows (W&T).

Square

Cast on 56 sts. K 5 rows, inc 13 sts evenly across on last (WS) row—69 sts. **Beg Chart Pat: Row 1** (RS) K3, work Chart Pat over 63 sts, k3. Keeping first and last 3 sts in garter st, cont working chart pat over center sts, through chart row 80. K 6 rows, dec 13 sts evenly across first row—56 sts. Bind off.

IN OTHER WORDS

1-to-3 inc [K1, yo, k1] in a st, wrap next st and turn (W&T), p3, W&T, k3.
1-to-5 inc [(K1, yo) twice, k1] in a st, W&T, p5, W&T, k5.
Acorn Cap St [K1, p1] twice, k1, W&T, p2, k1, p2, W&T, [k1, p1] twice, k1.
2/2 RC Sl 2 to cn, hold to back, k2; k2 from cn.
2/2 LC Sl 2 to cn, hold to front, k2; k2 from cn.
2/2 RPC Sl 2 to cn, hold to back, k2; p2 from cn.
2/2 LPC Sl 2 to cn, hold to front, p2; k2 from cn.
2/2 KPRC Sl 2 to cn, hold to back, k2; k1, p1 from cn.
2/2 KPLC Sl 2 to cn, hold to front, k1, p1; k2 from cn.
2/2 PKRC Sl 2 to cn, hold to back, k2; p1, k1 from cn.
2/2 PKLC Sl 2 to cn, hold to front, p1, k1; k2 from cn.
2/1/2 RPC Sl 3 to cn, hold to back, k2; p1 from cn (first st); k2 from cn.
2/1/2 LPC Sl 3 to cn, hold to front, k2; p1 from cn (first st); k2 from cn.

Chart Pat OVER 63 STS
Row 1 (RS) [P1, k1] 14 times, p1, 2/1/2 RPC, p1, [k1, p1] 14 times. *2 and all WS rows (except 6, 20, 22, 28, 30, 50, 52, 58, 60, and 68)* K the knit sts and M1P's and p the purl sts and yo's. *3* [K1, p1] 14 times, k3, p1, k3, [p1, k1] 14 times. *5* Rep row 1. *6* [K1, p1] 14 times, k1, p5, [k1, p1] 14 times, k1. *7* [K1, p1] 13 times, k1, 2/2 RC, k1, 2/2 LC, k1, [p1, k1] 13 times. *9* [P1, k1] 12 times, p1, 2/2 RC, k5, 2/2 LC, p1, [k1, p1] 12 times. *11* [K1, p1] 11 times, k1, 2/2 RC, k9, 2/2 LC, k1, [p1, k1] 11 times. *13* [P1, k1] 10 times, 2/1/2 RPC, k13, 2/1/2 LPC, [k1, p1] 10 times. *15* [K1, p1] 9 times, 2/2 RPC, p1, 2/2 LPC, k9, 2/2 RPC, p1, 2/2 LPC, [k1, p1] 9 times. *17* [P1, k1] 8 times, *2/2 RPC, p2, 1-to-5 inc, p2, 2/2 LPC*, k5, rep between *'s once, [k1, p1] 8 times. *19* [K1, p1] 7 times, *2/2 RPC, p4, k5, p4, 2/2 LPC*, k1, rep between *'s once, [p1, k1] 7 times. *20* [P1, k1] 7 times, p2, k17, p5, k17, p2, [k1, p1] 7 times. *21* [P1, k1] 5 times, p1, 2/1/2 RPC, [p6, Acorn Cap St, p6, 2/1/2 LPC] twice, p1, [k1, p1] 5 times. *22* [K1, p1] 6 times, p1, k1, [p2, k6, p2tog, k1, SSP, k6, p2, k1] twice, p2, k1, [p1, k1] 5 times. *23* [K1, p1] 4 times, k1, [2/2 RPC, p1, 2/2 LPC, p4, S2KP2, p4] twice, 2/2 RPC, p1, 2/2 LPC, k1, [p1, k1] 4 times. *25* [P1, k1] 3 times, p1, *2/2 RPC, p2, 1-to-5 inc, p2, 2/2 LPC*, p5, 2/2 RPC, p5, 2/2 LPC, p5, rep between *'s once, p1, [k1, p1] 3 times. *27* [K1, p1] twice, k1 *2/2 RPC, p4, k5, p4, 2/2 LPC*, p1, 2/2 RPC, p4, 1-to-3 inc, p4, 2/2 LPC, p1, rep between *'s once, k1, [p1, k1] twice. *28* [P1, k1] twice, p3, k17, p2, k1, p2, k6, p3, k6, p2, k1, p2, k17, p3, [k1, p1] twice. *29* P1, k1, p1, 2/2 RC, p6, Acorn Cap St, p6, 2/1/2 RPC, p6, k3, p6, 2/1/2 LPC, p6, Acorn Cap St, p6, 2/2 LC, p1, k1, p1. *30* K1, p1, k1, p4, *k6, p2tog, p1, SSP, k6*, p2, k1, p2, k6, p3, k6, p2, k1, p2, rep between *'s once, p4, k1, p1, k1. *31* K1, p1, k3, *2/2 LPC, p4, S2KP2, p4, 2/2 RPC*, p1, k2, p4, 1-to-3 inc, p1, k3, p1, 1-to-3 inc, p4, k2, p1, rep between *'s once, k3, p1, k1.
(Continued on page 63.)

Yarn color #2435

10cm/4"
28
20
• over stockinette stitch
(k on RS, p on WS)

• 4.5mm/US7, or size to obtain gauge

&

• cable needle (cn)
• st markers

This square originally appeared in Knitter's K45.

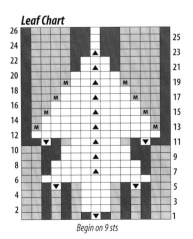

Leaf Chart

Begin on 9 sts

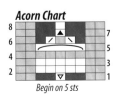

Acorn Chart

Begin on 5 sts

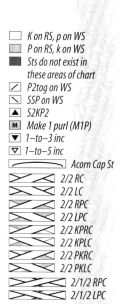

□ K on RS, p on WS
▨ P on RS, k on WS
■ Sts do not exist in
these areas of chart
╱ P2tog on WS
╲ SSP on WS
▲ S2KP2
Ⓜ Make 1 purl (M1P)
▼ 1–to–3 inc
▽ 1–to–5 inc
⌒ Acorn Cap St
⋈ 2/2 RC
⋈ 2/2 LC
⋈ 2/2 RPC
⋈ 2/2 LPC
⋈ 2/2 KPRC
⋈ 2/2 KPLC
⋈ 2/2 PKRC
⋈ 2/2 PKLC
⋈ 2/1/2 RPC
⋈ 2/1/2 LPC

Chart Pat

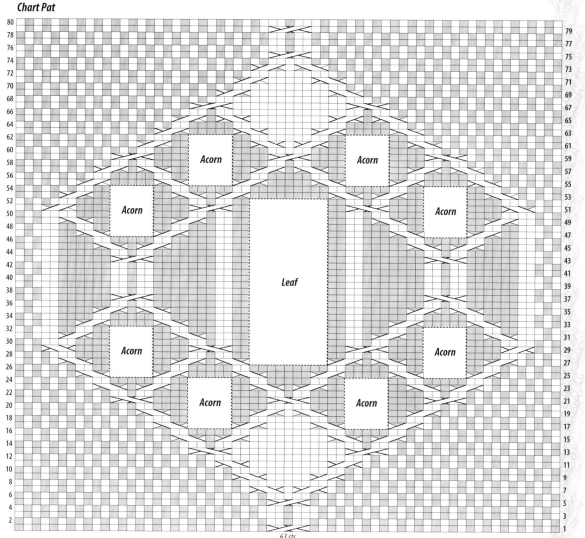

63 sts

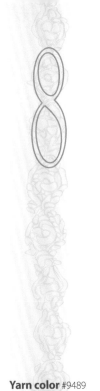

Kathy Zimmerman

LIGONIER, PENNSYLVANIA

I have been a knitter from the time I was a teenager and especially enjoy developing unique ribbing patterns, cables, and other stitch work.

I have been concentrating on what I call "composite cables." By that I mean that I select two or three cable stitch patterns and use elements of each to create a new, original stitch. In this square, the cable panels that border the center Irish Moss Staggered Diamonds combine an open cable with an enclosed cable variation.

Yarn color #9489

10cm/4"

28

20

• *over stockinette stitch (k on RS, p on WS)*

• 4.5mm/US 7, or size to obtain gauge

&

• cable needle (cn)

This square originally appeared in Knitter's K42.

Square
Cast on 56 sts. K 6 rows, inc 20 sts evenly across on last (RS) row—76 sts. **Beg Chart Pats: Row 1** (WS) K3, work 18 sts of Chart A, 34 sts of Chart B, 18 sts of Chart A, k3. Keeping first and last 3 sts in garter st, cont in chart pats as established over center 70 sts until chart rows 1–24 have been worked 3 times. K 5 rows, dec 20 sts on first row—56 sts. Bind off.

IN OTHER WORDS

2/1 RC Sl 1 to cn, hold to back, k2; k1 from cn.
2/1 LC Sl 2 to cn, hold to front, k1; k2 from cn.
2/1 RPC Sl 1 to cn, hold to back, k2; p1 from cn.
2/1 LPC Sl 2 to cn, hold to front, p1; k2 from cn.
2/2 RC Sl 2 to cn, hold to back, k2; k2 from cn.
2/2 LC Sl 2 to cn, hold to front, k2; k2 from cn.
2/2 RPC Sl 2 to cn, hold to back, k2; p2 from cn.
2/2 LPC Sl 2 to cn, hold to front, p2; k2 from cn.

Chart A *OVER 18 STS*
Rows 1 and 3 (WS) K3, p2, k8, p2, k3. **2** P3, k2, p8, k2, p3. **4** P3, 2/2 LPC, p4, 2/2 RPC, p3. **5** K5, p2, k4, p2, k5. **6** P5, 2/2 LC, 2/2 RC, p5. **7** K5, p8, k5. **8** P3, 2/2 RPC, 2/2 LC, 2/2 LPC, p3. **9, 11, 13, 15, 17, and 19** K3, p2, k2, p4, k2, p2, k3. **10, 14, and 18** P3, k2, p2, k4, p2, k2, p3. **12 and 16** P3, k2, p2, 2/2 LC, p2, k2, p3. **20** P3, 2/2 LPC, 2/2 LC, 2/2 RPC, p3. **21** Rep row 7. **22** P5, 2/2 RPC, 2/2 LPC, p5. **23** Rep row 5. **24** P3, 2/2 RPC, p4, 2/2 LPC, p3. Rep rows 1–24 for Chart A.

Chart B *OVER 34 STS*
Row 1 (WS) K1, *p2, [p1, k1] 4 times, p2,* k2, p4, k2, rep between *'s once, k1. **2** P1, *2/1 LPC, [p1, k1] 3 times, 2/1 RPC,* p2, 2/2 LC, p2, rep between *'s once, p1. **3** K2, *p2, [p1, k1] 3 times, p2,* k3, p4, k3, rep between *'s once, k2. **4** *P2, 2/1 LPC, [p1, k1] twice, 2/1 RPC, p2,* 2/1 RC, 2/1 LPC, rep between *'s once. **5** *K3, p2, [p1, k1] twice, p2, k3,* p2, k1, p3, rep between *'s once. **6** P3, *2/1 LPC, p1, k1, 2/1 RPC,* p2, 2/1 RC, p1, k1, 2/1 LPC, p2, rep between *'s once, p3. **7** K4, p3, k1, p2, k3, p2, [k1, p1] twice, p2, k3, p3, k1, p2, k4. **8** P4, 2/1 LPC, 2/1 RPC, p2, 2/1 RC, [p1, k1] twice, 2/1 LPC, p2, 2/1 LPC, 2/1 RPC, p4. **9** K5, p4, k3, p2, [k1, p1] 3 times, p2, k3, p4, k5. **10** P5, 2/2 LC, p2, 2/1 RC, [p1, k1] 3 times, 2/1 LPC, p2, 2/2 LC, p5. **11** K5, p4, k2, p2, [k1, p1] 4 times, p2, k2, p4, k5. **12** P5, k4, p2, k2, [p1, k1] 4 times, k2, p2, k4, p5. **13** K5, p4, k2, p2, [k1, p1] 4 times, p2, k2, p4, k5. **14** P5, 2/2 LC, p2, 2/1 LPC, [p1, k1] 3 times, 2/1 RPC, p2, 2/2 LC, p5. **15** K5, p4, k3, p2, [p1, k1] 3 times, p2, k3, p4, k5. **16** P4, 2/1 RC, 2/1 LPC, [p1, k1] twice, 2/1 RPC, p2, 2/1 RC, 2/1 LPC, p4. **17** K4, p2, k1, p3, k3, p2, [p1, k1] twice, p2, k3, p2, k1, p3, k4. **18** P3, *2/1 RC, p1, k1, 2/1 LPC,* p2, 2/1 LPC, p1, k1, 2/1 RPC, p2, rep between *'s once, p3. **19** K3, *p2, [k1, p1] twice, p2, k3,* p3, k1, p2, k3, rep between *'s once. **20** *P2, 2/1 RC, [p1, k1] twice, 2/1 LPC, p2,* 2/1 LPC, 2/1 RPC, rep between *'s once. **21** K2, *p2, [k1, p1] 3 times, p2,* k3, p4, k3, rep between *'s once, k2. **22** P1, *2/1 RC, [p1, k1] 3 times, 2/1 LPC,* p2, 2/2 LC, p2, rep between *'s once, p1. **23** K1, *p2, [k1, p1] 4 times, p2,* k2, p4, k2, rep between *'s once, k1. **24** P1, *k2, [p1, k1] 4 times, k2,* p2, k4, p2, rep between *'s once, p1. Rep rows 1–24 for Chart B.

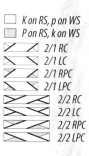

K on RS, p on WS
P on RS, k on WS
2/1 RC
2/1 LC
2/1 RPC
2/1 LPC
2/2 RC
2/2 LC
2/2 RPC
2/2 LPC

Chart A

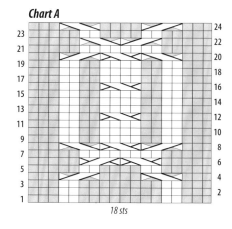

18 sts

Chart B

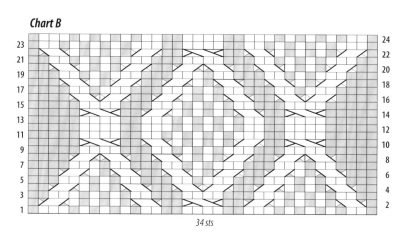

34 sts

Lily Chin
NEW YORK, NEW YORK

I've always enjoyed putting a new slant on things, and my bias square is a good example of this. The different construction here is underscored by the directional textures. There's nothing like putting a spin on things and turning design on its ear.

Yarn color #2440

10cm/4"

32

16

• over garter stitch (k every row)

• 4.5mm/US 7, or size to obtain gauge

This square originally appeared in Knitter's K42.

Notes

1 See *School*, page 60, for Make 1 knit (M1K) and purl (M1P), SSK and SSP. *2* Square is worked from corner to corner on the diagonal.

Square

Cast on 1 st. Work rows 1–134 of Chart Pat. Fasten off.

IN OTHER WORDS

Make bobble (MB) (*Note* Sl sts purlwise with yarn at WS of work.) [K1, yo, k1, yo, k1] in next st—5 sts. Turn, sl 1, p4. Turn, sl 1, k4. Turn, sl 1, p4. Turn, sl 1, [k2tog] twice, pass each of previous 2 sts over last st—1 st.

Chart Pat

Row 1 (RS) KOK in st on needle—3 sts. ***2 and 4*** Knit. ***3*** K1, KOK, k1—5 sts. ***5*** K1, M1K, k3, M1K, k1—7 sts. ***6*** K2, [p1, k1] twice, k1. ***7*** K1, M1K, [p1 irb, k1] twice, p1 irb, M1K, k1—9 sts. ***8*** K1, p1, k1, *p1 irb, k1; rep from * to last 2 sts, p1, k1. ***9*** K1, M1P, *k1, p1 irb; rep from * to last 2 sts, k1, M1P, k1. ***10*** K2, *p1 irb, k1; rep from * to last st, k1. ***11*** K1, M1K, *p1 irb, k1; rep from * to last 2 sts, p1 irb, M1K, k1. ***12*** Rep row 8. ***13*** Rep row 9. ***14*** Rep row 10. ***15, 17, 19, and 21*** K1, M1K, k to last st, M1K, k1. ***16, 18, and 20*** Knit. ***22*** P1, *p2tog, yo; rep from * to last 2 sts, p2. ***23–29*** Rep rows 15–21—31 sts. ***30*** *K3, MB; rep from*, end k3. ***31–45*** Rep rows 15–29—47 sts. ***46–52*** Rep rows 8–14—53 sts. ***53–67*** Rep rows 15–29—69 sts. ***68*** K2, MB, *k3, MB; rep from*, end k2. ***69, 71, 73, and 75*** K1, k2tog, k to last 3 sts, SSK, k1. ***70, 72, and 74*** Knit. ***76*** Rep row 22. ***77–83*** Rep rows 69–75—53 sts. ***84*** K2, *p1 irb, k1; rep from * to last st, k1. ***85*** K1, k2tog, *p1 irb, k1; rep from * to last 4 sts, p1 irb, SSK, k1. ***86*** Rep row 8. ***87*** K1, p2tog, *k1, p1 irb; rep from * to last 4 sts, k1, SSP, k1. ***88*** Rep row 10. ***89*** Rep row 85. ***90*** Rep row 8. ***91–105*** Rep rows 69–83—31 sts. ***106*** Rep row 30. ***107–128*** Rep rows 69–90—9 sts. ***129–132*** Rep rows 69–72—5 sts. ***133*** K1, k3tog, k1—3 sts. ***134*** K3tog.

PURL IN ROW BELOW (p1 irb)

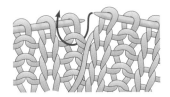

Purl stitch in row below next stitch on left needle.

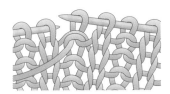

Drop stitch from left needle.

KOK INCREASE (k1-yo-k1)

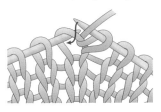

1 Knit 1, leaving stitch on left needle.
2 Bring yarn to front and over needle.
3 Knit into the stitch again.

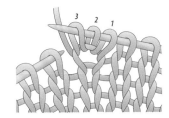

Completed increase: 3 stitches from 1 stitch.

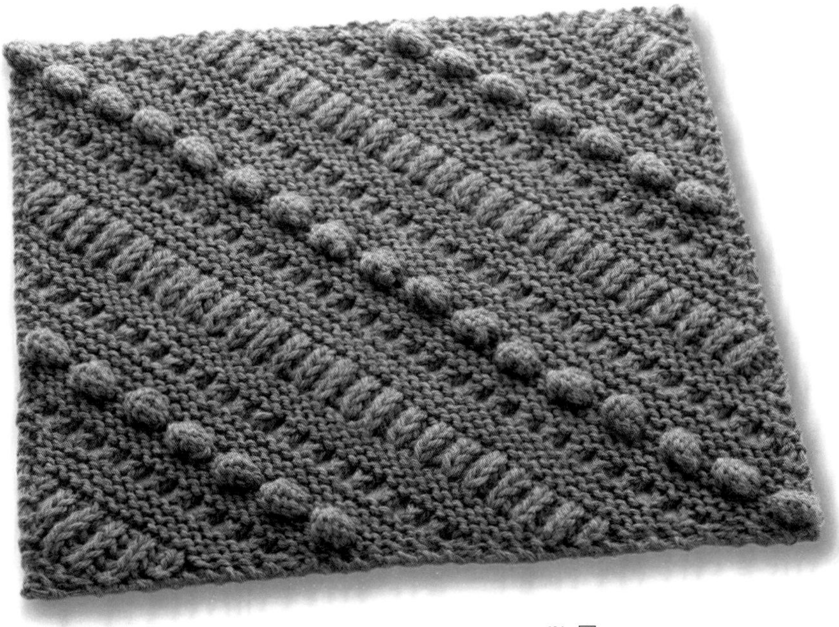

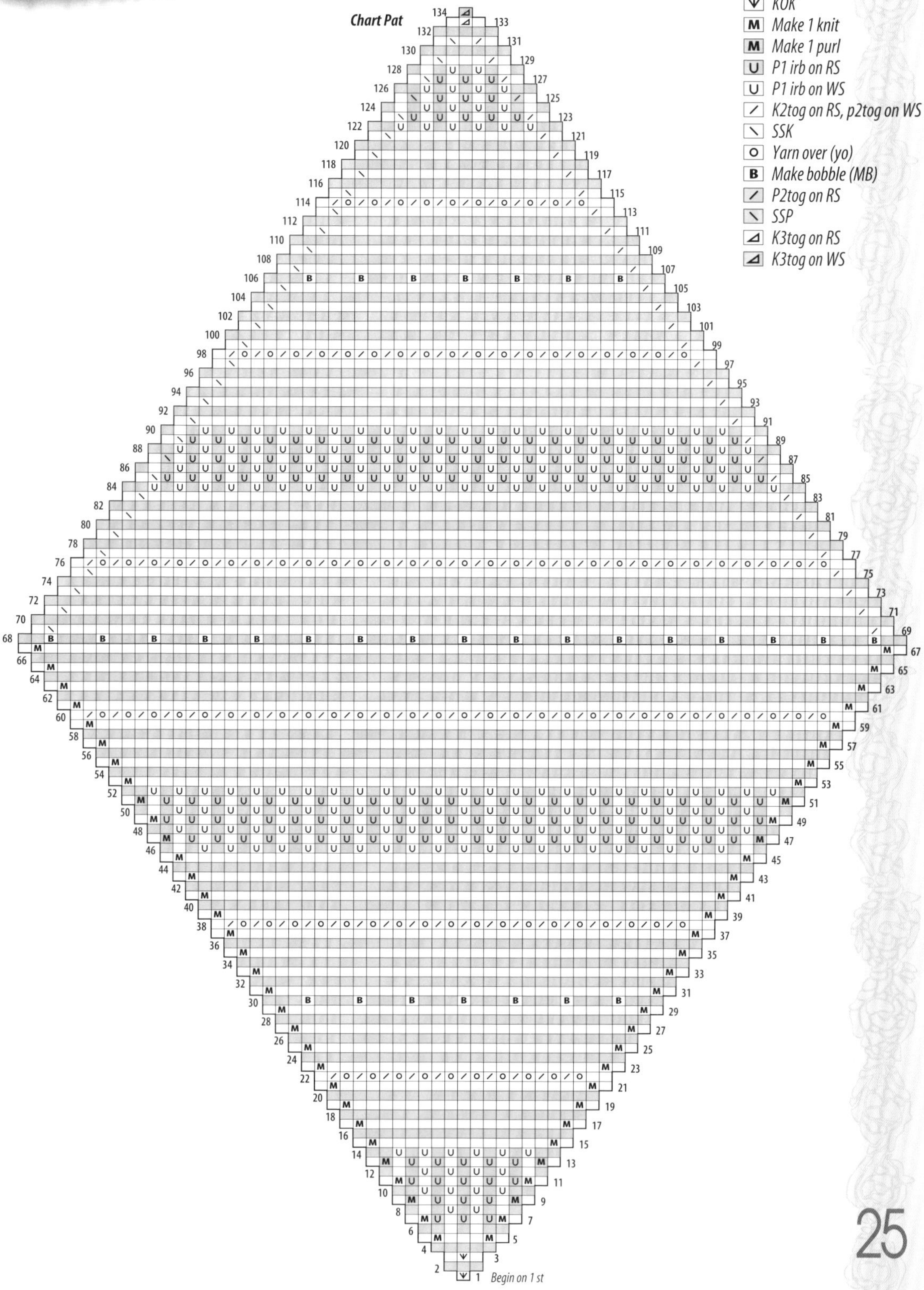

Chart Pat
Begin on 1 st

□	K on RS, p on WS
▒	P on RS, k on WS
V	KOK
M	Make 1 knit
M	Make 1 purl
U	P1 irb on RS
U	P1 irb on WS
/	K2tog on RS, p2tog on WS
\	SSK
O	Yarn over (yo)
B	Make bobble (MB)
/	P2tog on RS
\	SSP
◿	K3tog on RS
◿	K3tog on WS

Wendy Sacks
BROOKLYN, NEW YORK

For me, a hand-knitting project must have enough variation to keep it interesting, but not be so complex that it requires constant referral to the instructions.

Tucking tends to spread the fabric. When used with ribbing, which draws the fabric in, the resulting stitch has a flowing quality reminiscent of Art Nouveau design—one of my favorite periods in the decorative arts. The cable panel with alternating crosses and bobbles adds more texture—and makes it fun to knit!

Yarn color #2445

10cm/4"

28

20

• over stockinette stitch (k on RS, p on WS)

• 4.5mm/US7, or size to obtain gauge

&

• cable needle (cn)

This square originally appeared in Knitter's K45.

Square

Cast on 56 sts. K 5 rows, inc 14 sts evenly across last (WS) row—70 sts. **Preparation row** (RS) K3, [k2, p2] 6 times, k2, [p1, k1] twice, k1, p2, k2, p1, k1, p1, [k2, p2] 6 times, k5. **Beg Charts A and B: Row 1** (WS) K3, work Chart A over 26 sts, Chart B over 12 sts, Chart A over 26 sts, k3. Keeping first and last 3 sts in garter st, cont in chart pat as established over center 64 sts until piece measures 11¼" from beg, end with a WS row. K 6 rows, dec 14 sts evenly across first row—56 sts. Bind off.

IN OTHER WORDS

Make bobble (MB) (K1, p1) twice into st. Pass 4th, 3rd, 2nd over first st on needle.

Cable 1 Sl 4 sts to cn, hold to front, k2; sl 2 p sts from cn back to left needle and place cn with 2 k sts behind work (to left of working yarn); p2 from needle, k2 from cn.

Cable 2 Sl 4 sts to cn and hold to front, k2; sl 2 p sts from cn to left needle and p2; k2 from cn.

CHART A *OVER 26 STS*

Rows 1 and 3 (WS) [P2, k2] 6 times, p2. **2 and 4** [K2, p2] 6 times, k2. **5 and 7** P2, k6, [p2, k2] twice, p2, k6, p2. **6** K2, p6, [k2, p2] twice, k2, p6, k2. **8** K2, TS, p4, TS, [k2, p2] twice, k2, TS, p4, TS, k2. **9** Rep row 5. **10 and 12** Rep row 6. **11** P2, k1, TS, k2, TS, k1, [p2, k2] twice, p2, k1, TS, k2, TS, k1, p2. **13 and 15** Rep row 1. **14 and 16** Rep row 2. **17, 19, and 21** [P2, k2] twice, p2, k6, [p2, k2] twice, p2. **18 and 22** [K2, p2] twice, k2, p6, [k2, p2] twice, k2. **20** [K2, p2] twice, k2, TS, p4, TS, [k2, p2] twice, k2. **23** [P2, k2] twice, p2, k1, TS, k2, TS, k1, [p2, k2] twice, p2. **24** Rep row 18. Rep rows 1–24 for Chart A.

CHART B *OVER 12 STS*

Row 1 and all WS rows K1, p1, k1, p2, k2, p2, k1, p1, k1. **2, 6, 10, and 14** P1, MB, p1, k2, p2, k2, p1, MB, p1. **4** P1, k1, p1, work Cable 1 over 6 sts, p1, k1, p1. **8** P1, k1, p1, k2, p2, k2, p1, k1, p1. **12** P1, k1, p1, work Cable 2 over 6 sts, p1, k1, p1. **16** Rep row 8. Rep rows 1–16 for Chart B.

TUCK STITCH (TS) (on a RS row)

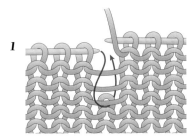

1

Slip stitch off left needle and drop it down 3 rows. Replace stitch and 3 strands on left needle (as shown).

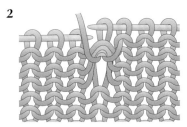

2

Purl through stitch and strands. (On a WS row, knit instead of purl, on step 2.)

☐ K on RS, p on WS
☐ P on RS, k on WS
B Make bobble (MB)
T Tuck Stitch (TS)
⬤⬤ Cable 2
⬤⬤ Cable 1

Chart A

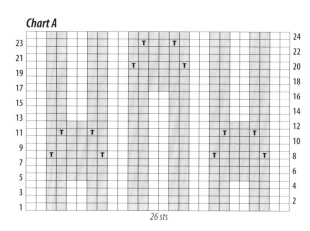

| | | | | | | | | | | | | | | | | | | | | | | | | |
24
23 | | | | | | | | T | | T | | | | | | | | | | | | | | 24
21 | | | | | | | | | | | | | | | | | | | | | | | | | | 22
19 | | | | | | | | T | | | T | | | | | | | | | | | | | 20
17 | | | | | | | | | | | | | | | | | | | | | | | | | | 18
15 | | | | | | | | | | | | | | | | | | | | | | | | | | 16
13 | | | | | | | | | | | | | | | | | | | | | | | | | | 14
11 | | | | | T | | T | | | | | | | | T | | T | | | | | | 12
9 | | | T | | | T | | | | | | | | T | | | T | | | | | | 10
7 | | | | | | | | | | | | | | | | | | | | | | | | | | 8
5 | | | | | | | | | | | | | | | | | | | | | | | | | | 6
3 | | | | | | | | | | | | | | | | | | | | | | | | | | 4
1 | | | | | | | | | | | | | | | | | | | | | | | | | | 2

26 sts

Chart B

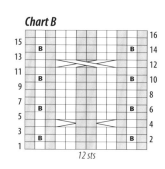

| | | | | | | | | | | | |
16
15 | | B | | | | | | | B | | 16
13 | | | | | | | | | | | | 14
11 | | ⬤⬤ | | | | | | | | 12
9 | | B | | | | | | | B | | 10
7 | | | | | | | | | | | | 8
5 | | B | | | | | | | B | | 6
3 | | | ⬤ | | | ⬤ | | | | 4
1 | | B | | | | | | | B | | 2

12 sts

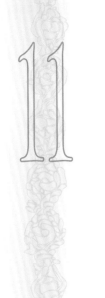

Melissa Leapman
NEW YORK, NEW YORK

To me, knitting and crocheting are perfect blends of creative expression, technical know-how, and time-honored tradition. Taking a seemingly-shapeless, yet malleable strand of yarn and manipulating it into something beautiful, warm, and useful surely is a magical transformation.

This afghan square typifies my work through its use of a variety of textures. For example, traveling stitches and the juxtaposition of knit and purl stitches define the legs and tail of the cat. Many of my favorite designs use this technique, mingling interesting textures into fun-to-knit and easy-to-wear garments. Besides, a ball of yarn without a cat is like a knitter without needles!

Yarn color #9408

10cm/4"
26
18
• over stockinette stitch
(k on RS, p on WS)

• 5mm/US 8, or size to obtain gauge

• cable needle (cn)
• st markers

This square originally appeared in Knitter's K43.

Note
See *School*, page 60, for SSK.

Square
Cast on 56 sts. K 5 rows, inc 2 sts on last row—58 sts. **Beg Chart Pat: Row 1** (RS) K3, p3, place marker (pm), work Chart Pat over 42 sts, pm, p7, k3. **Row 2** K to marker, work Chart Pat between markers, k to end. Cont working Chart Pat between markers, and sts outside markers in garter st and reverse St st as established, through chart row 67. K 5 rows, dec 2 sts on first row—56 sts. Bind off.

IN OTHER WORDS
1-to-3 inc [K1, p1, k1] in 1 st.
1-to-5 inc [K1, p1, k1, p1, k1] in 1 st.
6-to-1 dec Sl 4, *pass 2nd st on right needle over first, sl st back to left needle and pass 2nd st over it; sl st back to right needle; rep from* once more, end pass 2nd st over first.
1/1 LC Sl 1 to cn, hold to front, k1; k1 from cn.
1/1 RC Sl 1 to cn, hold to back, k1; k1 from cn.
1/1 LPC Sl 1 to cn, hold to front, p1; k1 from cn.
1/1 RPC Sl 1 to cn, hold to back, k1; p1 from cn.
1/2 LC Sl 1 to cn, hold to front, k2; k1 from cn.
1/2 RC Sl 2 to cn, hold to back, k1; k2 from cn.
3/1 LPC Sl 3 to cn, hold to front, p1; k3 from cn.
3/2 LPC Sl 3 to cn, hold to front, p2; k3 from cn.

Chart Pat *BEGIN ON 42 STS*
(**Note** Sl sts purlwise with yarn in back.)
Row 1 (RS) P42. **2** K42. **3** P12, 1-to-5 inc, p29—46 sts. **4** K29, p5, k12. **5** P12, k5, p6, 1-to-5 inc, p22—50 sts. **6** K22, p5, k6, p5, k12. **7** P12, k3, k2tog, p6, k5, p14, 1-to-5 inc, p7—53 sts. **8** K7, p5, k14, p5, k6, p4, k12. **9** P12, k2, k2tog, p6, k3, k2tog, p14, k5, p7—51 sts. **10** K7, p5, k14, p4, k6, p3, k12. **11** P12, k3, p6, k2, k2tog, p13, 1-to-3 inc, sl 1, k2, k2tog, p7. **12** K7, p7, k13, p3, k6, p3, k12. **13** P12, k3, p6, k3, p13, k3, sl 1, k1, k2tog, p7—50 sts. **14** K7, p6, k13, p3, k6, p3, k12. **15** P12, k3, p6, k3, p13, k3, sl 1, k2, p7. **16** Rep row 14. **17** P12, k2, 1/1 LC, p5, k3, p13, k3, sl 1, k2, p7. **18** K7, p6, k13, p3, k5, p4, k12. **19** P12, k3, 1/1 LC, p4, k3, p13, k3, sl 1, k2, p7. **20** K7, p6, k13, p3, k4, p5, k12.

21 P11, 1/1 RC, k3, 1/1 LC, p2, 1/1 RC, k2, p13, k3, sl 1, k2, p7. **22** K7, p6, k13, p4, k2, p7, k11. **23** P10, 1/1 RC, k5, 1/2 LC, k4, p13, k3, sl 1, k2, p7. **24** K7, p6, k13, p14, k10. **25** P10, k9, 1/2 LC, k2, p13, k3, sl 1, k2, p7. **26** Rep row 24. **27** P9, 1/1 RC, k10, 1/2 LC, p12, 1/1 RC, k1, 1/1 RC, k2, p7. **28** K7, p7, k12, p15, k9. **29** P9, k14, 1/2 LC, p9, 1/1 RC, k1, 1/1 RC, k3, p7. **30** K7, p8, k3, p23, k9. **31** P8, 1/1 RC, k26, 1/2 RC, k4, p7. **32** K7, p35, k8. **33** P8, k34, 1/1 LC, p6. **34** K6, p36, k8. **35** P8, k36, p6. **36** Rep row 34. **37** P8, 1/1 LPC, k34, p6. **38** K6, p35, k9. **39** P9, k35, p6. **40** Rep row 38. **41** P9, 1/1 LPC, k33, p6. **42** K6, p34, k10. **43** P10, k3, 1/1 RPC, p11, k18, p6. **44** K6, p15, k15, p4, k10. **45** P10, k4, p19, k5, 1/2 RC, 1/2 LC, p6. **46** K6, p7, k23, p4, k10. **47** P10, k4, p23, 1/1 RC, k4, 1/1 LC, p5. **48** K5, p8, k23, p4, k10. **49** P9, 1/1 RC, k1, 1/1 RPC, p22, 1/1 RC, k6, 1/1 LC, p4. **50** K4, p10, k23, p4, k9. **51** P9, k4, p23, k10, p4. **52** Rep row 50. **53** P9, k4, p22, 1/1 RC, k8, 1/1 LC, p3. **54** K3, p12, k22, p4, k9. **55** P8, 1/1 RC, k1, 1/1 RPC, p22, k12, p3. **56** K3, p12, k23, p4, k8. **57** P8, k4, p23, k3, 1/1 RC, k2, 1/1 LC, k3, p3. **58** Rep row 56. **59** P2, 1-to-3 inc, p4, 1/1 RC, k1, 1/1 RPC, p23, k2, 1/1 RPC, p4, 1/1 LPC, k2, p3—52 sts. **60** K3, p3, k6, p3, k24, p4, k4, p3, k2. **61** P2, 3/1 LPC, p3, k2, 1/1 RPC, p24, k1, k2tog, p6, SSK, k1, p3—50 sts. **62** K3, p2, k6, p2, k25, [p3, k3] twice. **63** P3, 3/2 LPC, 1/1 RC, k2tog, p25, k2tog, p6, SSK, p3—47 sts. **64** K36, p6, k5. **65** P5, 6-to-1 dec, p36—42 sts. **66** K42. **67** P42.

□ K on RS, p on WS
▨ P on RS, k on WS
↘ SSK
↗ K2tog
▽ Sl 1 purlwise with yarn in back
■ Sts do not exist in these areas of chart
▽ 1-to-3 inc
▼ 1-to-5 inc
▲ 6-to-1 dec
⟋⟍ 1/1 LC
⟍⟋ 1/1 RC
⟍⟋ 1/1 LPC
⟋⟍ 1/1 RPC
⟋⟋ 1/2 LC
⟍⟍ 1/2 RC
⟋ 3/1 LPC
⟍ 3/2 LPC

Chart Pat

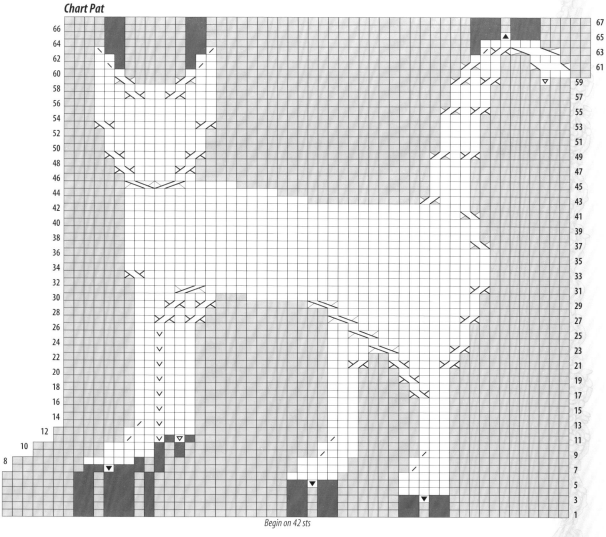

Begin on 42 sts

Bette Anne Lampers

SNOHOMISH, WASHINGTON

My mom taught me to knit when I was about seven, although I don't remember her knitting very much herself. I started designing my own patterns in my teens. I have tried many other handicrafts, but I always come back to knitting—it is so therapeutic.

This afghan square is representative of a swatch I used in calculating the sizing for the "Skill-building entrelac" cardigan seen in a previous issue of Knitter's magazine [K44].

Yarn color #2440

10cm/4"
28
19
• over stockinette stitch
(k on RS, p on WS)

• 4.5mm/US 7, or size to obtain gauge

&
• cable needle (cn)
• tapestry needle

This square originally appeared in Knitter's K46.

Notes

1 See *School*, page 60, for cable cast-on, knit into front and back of st (kf&b), SK2P, SP2P, S2KP2, and SSK. *2* Sl sts purlwise. On RS rows, sl st with yarn in back; on WS rows, sl st with yarn in front. *3* On two of the square's four corners, a diagonal line of "chain stitch" forms naturally. After the square is finished, work a line of embroidered chain stitch in the other two corners. *4* Turn work after every row, unless instructed otherwise.

MOSS ST (MS)

Row 1 *K1, p1; rep from*. *2 and 4* K the knit sts and p the purl sts. *3* *P1, k1; rep from*. Rep rows 1–4 for Moss st.

ENTRELAC SEQUENCE

Two base triangles Cast on 2 sts. **Next row** (RS) K2. **Next row** (WS) Sl 1, p1. **Next row** Cast on 1 st using cable cast-on and leave new st on right needle, p1, k1. **Next row** Sl 1, k1, p1. **Next row** Cast on 1 st as before, p1, k2. **Next row** Sl 1, p1, k1, p1. Cont in this way, casting on 1 st at beg of every RS row (working incs into MS pat), slipping first st of every WS row and knitting last st of every RS row until there are 17 sts, end with a WS row*—1 base triangle complete. Cast on 2 sts onto left needle (with first base triangle). Rep between *'s once more—2 base triangles complete.

First right-side triangle: Next row (RS) P1, k1. **Next row** Sl 1, k1. **Next row** K into front and back of first st (kf&b), SSK (last st tog with first st of base triangle). **Next row** Sl 1, p1, k1. **Next row** Kf&b, k1, SSK. **Next row** Sl 1, p1, k1, p1. Cont in this way, working kf&b at beg and SSK at end of every RS row, and keeping in MS pat until there are 17 sts on right needle and all sts from 1 base triangle edge have been worked, ending with a RS row. Do not turn.

Chart A rectangle Cont with RS facing, pick up and k 17 sts along rem edge of base triangle. Work Chart A for 34 rows, and all sts of next base triangle have been worked. Do not turn.

First left-side triangle Cont with RS facing, pick up and k 17 sts along rem edge of base triangle. **Next row** (WS) Work 17 sts in MS pat. **Next row** Sl 1, work in pat over 14 sts, k2tog. **Next row** Work even in MS pat. **Next row** Sl 1, work in pat over 13 sts, k2tog. Cont in this way, working dec at end of every RS row, until 1 st rem. **Chart B rectangle** With WS facing, pick up and p 16

sts along triangle just worked—17 sts. Work Chart B for 34 rows, and all sts of Chart A rectangle have been worked, ending with a WS row. Do not turn.

Chart C rectangle Cont with WS facing, pick up and p 17 sts along rem edge of Chart A rectangle. Work Chart C for 34 rows, and all sts of right-side triangle have been worked.

Second right-side triangle Work as for first right-side triangle. Do not turn.

Chart D rectangle Cont with RS facing, pick up and k 17 sts along rem Chart C edge. Work Chart D for 34 rows, and all sts of Chart B rectangle have been worked. Do not turn.

Second left-side triangle Cont with RS facing, pick up and k 17 sts along rem edge of Chart B rectangle. Work as for first left-side triangle.

Top-edge triangles With WS facing, pick up and p 16 sts along triangle just worked—17 sts. *Next row* (RS) Work 17 sts in MS pat. *Next row* Sl 1, work in pat over 15 sts, p2tog. *Next row* Sl 1, work in pat to last 2 sts, k2tog. *Next row* Sl 1, work in pat over 12 sts, p2tog. Cont in this way, until 3 sts rem. SP2P*—1 top-edge triangle complete. With WS facing, pick up and p 16 sts along rem edge of Chart D rectangle—17 sts. Rep from * to * once—2 top-edge triangles complete. Fasten off last st.

Garter stitch border With RS facing, pick up and k 53 sts along top edge of square. K 5 rows. Bind off leaving last st on needle, then pick up and k 55 more sts along left side edge. K 5 rows. Bind off leaving last st, pick up and k 55 more sts along bottom edge. K 5 rows. Bind off leaving last st on needle, then pick up and k 59 more sts along right side edge. K 5 rows. Bind off all sts.

IN OTHER WORDS

5-to-3 dec SSK, k1, k2tog.
Make bobble (MB) [K1, p1, k1] in same st, turn, sl 1, p2, turn; sl 1, k2, turn; sl 1, p2, turn; SK2P.
1-to-5 inc [K1, p1, k1, p1, k1] into 1 st.
1/2 RPC Sl 2 to cn, hold to back, k1; p2 from cn.
1/2 Rib RC Sl 2 to cn, hold to back, k1; [p1, k1] from cn.
1/3 RC Sl 3 to cn, hold to back, k1; k3 from cn.
1/3 LC Sl 1 to cn, hold to front, k3; k1 from cn.
3/6 Rib RC Sl 6 to cn, hold to back, k1, p1, k1; [p1, k1] 3 times from cn.
(Continued on page 63.)

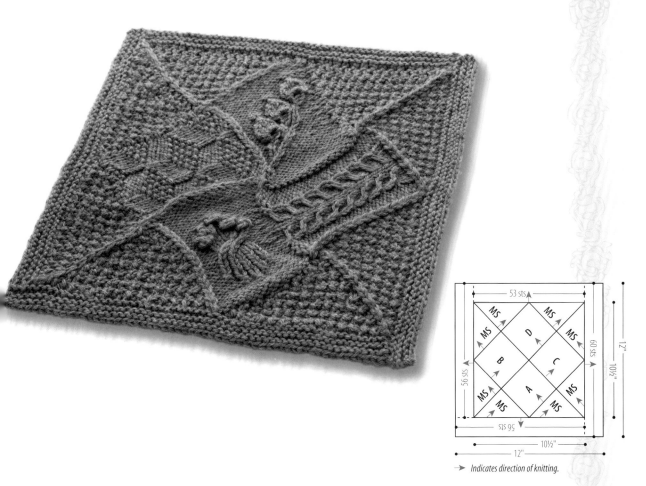

53 sts

MS MS MS MS
D
B C
MS MS
A
MS MS MS MS

56 sts
60 sts
56 sts
56 sts

12"
10½"

12"
10½"

→ Indicates direction of knitting.

Chart A

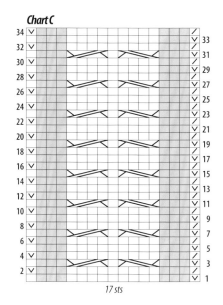

17 sts

Chart B

17 sts

☐ K on RS, p on WS
▨ P on RS, k on WS
∨ Sl 1 purlwise with yarn at WS of work
◸ SSK on RS rows
   (last st of triangle or
   rectangle with first st of next)
◿ P2tog on WS
   (last st of triangle or
   rectangle with first st of next)
△ 5-to-3 dec
▲ S2KP2
B Make bobble (MB)
3 P3 on WS
5 K5 on RS, p5 on WS
⬓ 1-to-5 inc
⧄ 1/2 RPC
⧄ 1/2 Rib RC
⧄ 1/3 RC
⧄ 1/3 LC
▱ 3/6 Rib RC

Chart C

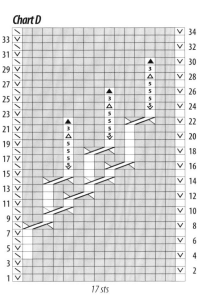

17 sts

Chart D

17 sts

CHAIN STITCH

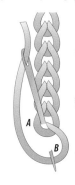

A
B

31

Working From Charts

Charts are graphs or grids of squares that represent the right side of knitted fabric. They illustrate every stitch and the relationship between the rows of stitches. Squares contain knitting symbols. The key defines each symbol as an operation to make a stitch or stitches. The pattern provides any special instructions for using the chart(s) or the key. The numbers along the sides of charts indicate the rows. A number on the right marks a right-side row that is worked leftward from the number. A number on the left marks a wrong-side row that is worked rightward. Since many stitches are worked differently on wrong-side rows, the key will indicate that. If the pattern is worked circularly, all rows are right-side rows and worked from right to left. Bold lines within the graph represent repeats. These set off a group of stitches that are repeated across a row. You begin at the edge of a row or where the pattern indicates for the required size, work across to the second line, then repeat the stitches between the repeat lines as many times as directed, and finish the row.

Chart for Square 5, page 16

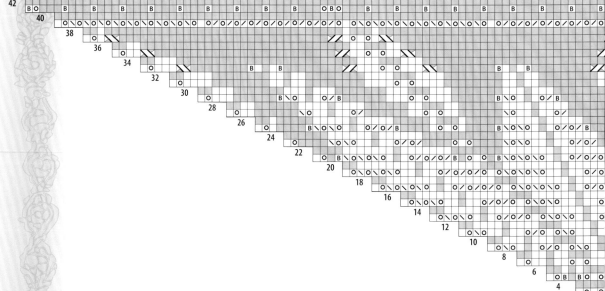

Chart Pat

Chart Pat

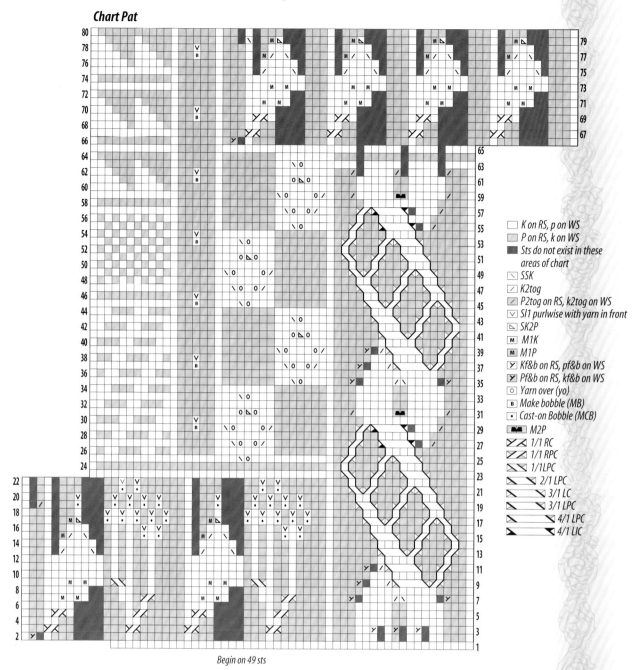

Begin on 49 sts

Legend (upper chart):

☐ K on RS, p on WS
▨ P on RS, k on WS
■ Sts do not exist in these areas of chart
◲ SSK
◱ K2tog
◲ P2tog on RS, k2tog on WS
◡ Sl1 purlwise with yarn in front
◳ SK2P
Ⓜ M1K
Ⓜ M1P
⬀ Kf&b on RS, pf&b on WS
⬁ Pf&b on RS, kf&b on WS
○ Yarn over (yo)
Ⓑ Make bobble (MB)
• Cast-on Bobble (MCB)
▰▰ M2P
⤫ 1/1 RC
⤫ 1/1 RPC
⤫ 1/1LPC
⬂ 2/1 LPC
⬃ 3/1 LC
⬃ 3/1 LPC
⬃ 4/1 LPC
⬃ 4/1 LIC

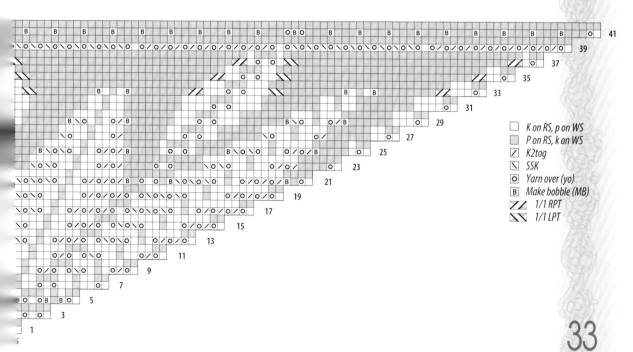

Legend (lower chart):

☐ K on RS, p on WS
▨ P on RS, k on WS
◱ K2tog
◲ SSK
○ Yarn over (yo)
Ⓑ Make bobble (MB)
⤫ 1/1 RPT
⤫ 1/1 LPT

Nicky Epstein
NEW YORK, NEW YORK

Appliqué and dimensional knitting have become important design techniques for me. Knitter's was one of the first to show and regularly publish my designs using this technique. When they asked me to do a square for The Great American Afghan, I chose appliqué.

Note
See *School*, page 60, for cable cast-on, SSK and SK2P.

Square
With MC, cast on 55 sts. K 5 rows. * **Next row** (RS) Knit. **Next row** K3, p to last 3 sts, k3. Rep from * until piece measures 11¼" from beg, end with a RS row. K 5 rows. Bind off.

Trees (Make 1 in each of 3 colors)
Cast on 7 sts. Work rows 1–63 of Chart Pat. Fasten off.

Finishing
Block pieces. Sew trees to square, using photo as guide for placement.

IN OTHER WORDS
Chart Pat *BEG ON 7 STS*
Rows 1, 3 and 5 (RS) [K1, p1] 3 times, k1. **2, 4, and 6** [P1, k1] 3 times, p1. **7** Cable cast on 12 sts, then k these 12 sts, k7—19 sts. **8** Cable cast on 12 sts, then p these 12 sts, p19—31 sts. **9** K13, k2tog, yo, k1, yo, SSK, k13. **10 and all foll WS rows (except 28 and 44)** Purl. **11** K1, k2tog, k10, k2tog, yo, k1, yo, SSK, k10, SSK, k1—29 sts. **13** K1, k2tog, k9,

Yarn color
MC #9445
A #2445
B #2452

10cm/4"
24
18
• over stockinette stitch (k on RS, p on WS)

• 5mm/US 8, or size to obtain gauge

This square originally appeared in Knitter's K42.

Chart Pat

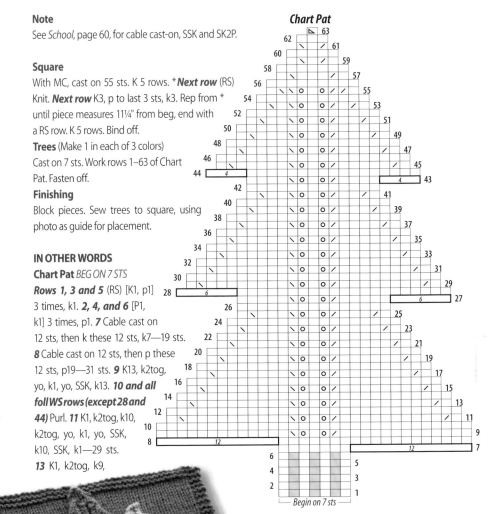

Begin on 7 sts

□ K on RS, p on WS
▧ P on RS, k on WS
╱ K2tog
╲ SSK
◉ Yarn over (yo)
◣ SK2P
▭ # Cable cast on the # of sts indicated, then k (on RS rows) or p (on WS rows) these sts

k2tog, yo, k1, yo, SSK, k9, SSK, k1—27 sts. **15** K1, k2tog, k8, k2tog, yo, k1, yo, SSK, k8, SSK, k1—25 sts. **17** K1, k2tog, k7, k2tog, yo, k1, yo, SSK, k7, SSK, k1—23 sts. **19** K1, k2tog, k6, k2tog, yo, k1, yo, SSK, k6, SSK, k1—21 sts. **21** K1, k2tog, k5, k2tog, yo, k1, yo, SSK, k5, SSK, k1—19 sts. **23** K1, k2tog, k4, k2tog, yo, k1, yo, SSK, k4, SSK, k1—17 sts. **25** K1, k2tog, k3, k2tog, yo, k1, yo, SSK, k3, SSK, k1—15 sts. **27** Cable cast on and k6 sts, k5, k2tog, yo, k1, yo, SSK, k5—21 sts. **28** Cable cast on and p6 sts, p21—27 sts. **29–40** Rep rows 15–26—15 sts. **41** K1, k2tog, k2, k2tog, yo, k1, yo, SSK, k2, SSK, k1—13 sts. **43** Cable cast on and k4 sts, k4, k2tog, yo, k1, yo, SSK, k4—17 sts. **44** Cable cast on and p4 sts, p17—21 sts. **45–50** Rep rows 21–26—15 sts. **51** K1, k2tog, k2, k2tog, yo, k1, yo, SSK, k2, SSK, k1—13 sts. **53** [K1, k2tog] twice, yo, k1, yo, [SSK, k1] twice—11 sts. **55** K1, [k2tog] twice, yo, k1, yo, [SSK] twice, k1—9 sts. **57** K1, k2tog, k3, SSK, k1—7 sts. **59** K1, k2tog, k1, SSK, k1—5 sts. **61** K2tog, k1, SSK—3 sts. **63** SK2P.

Sidna Farley
DENVER, COLORADO

With little to no desire, I was introduced to knitting by an exchange student living with us. My knitting was so tight, I poked a hole in my finger with the knitting needle and promptly gave it up. However, my younger sister did learn to knit, and looking at her growing pile of sweaters, I said to myself, "If my stupid sister can knit, so can I."—And so I could!

When I first saw the charts for Tvaandsstickat (Scandinavian 2-end knitting), I thought the method was done just with slip stitches as in this pattern. I decided to try out my theory; this square is the result. It allows you to use the 2-end patterns and produce a garment that isn't double thick. It's easier and speedier to knit. I chose this for my square because it feels like my "unvention."

Yarn color #2435

10cm/4"
28
18
• over stockinette st
(k on RS, p on WS)

• 5mm/US 8,
or size to obtain gauge

&
• St markers

This square originally appeared in Knitter's K42.

Square

Cast on 55 sts. K 5 rows, dec 2 sts on last row—53 sts. * **Next row** (RS) Knit. **Next row** K3, p47, k3. Rep from * twice more. **Beg Chart Pat: Row 1** (RS) K7, place marker (pm), work Chart Pat over 39 sts, pm, k7. **Row 2** K3, p4, work Chart Pat over 39 sts, p4, k3. Cont in pat as established through chart row 65. * **Next row** (WS) K3, p47, k3. **Next row** Knit. Rep from * twice more, inc 2 sts on last (RS) row—55 sts. K 5 rows. Bind off.

IN OTHER WORDS

Chart Pat *OVER 39 STS*
(**Note** Sl sts purlwise with yarn in front.)
Row 1 (RS) K4, p1, [k5, p1] 5 times, k4. **2 and all WS rows** Purl. **3** [K3, p1, sl 1, p1] 6 times, k3. **5** K2, *[p1, sl 1] twice, p1, k1, [p1, sl 1] twice, p1 *, p1, sl 1, p1, k1, p1, sl 1, p1, k3, rep between *'s once, k2. **7** K1, *p1, sl 1, p1, k1, [p1, sl 1] twice, p1, k1, p1, sl 1, p1 *, k3, [p1, sl 1] twice, p1, k3, rep between *'s once, k1. **9** [P1, sl 1, p1, k3] 6 times, p1, sl 1, p1. **11** K1, *p1, sl 1, [p1, k3] twice, p1, sl 1, p1 *, k3, [p1, sl 1] twice, p1, k3, rep between *'s once, k1. **13** K2, *p1, sl 1, p1, k5, p1, sl 1, p1 *, k3, p1, sl 1, p1, k1, p1, sl 1, p1, k3, rep between *'s once, k2. **15** Rep row 3. **17** K1, *k3, p1, sl 1, p1, k1, p1, sl 1, p1, k3 *, [p1, sl 1] twice, p1, k1, [p1, sl 1] twice, p1, rep between *'s once, k1. **19** K1, *p1, k3, [p1, sl 1] twice, p1, k3, p1 *, sl 1, p1, k1, [p1, sl 1] twice, p1, k1, p1, sl 1, rep between *'s once, k1. **21** Rep row 9. **23** Rep row 11. **25** Rep row 13. **27** Rep row 3. **29** K2, *[p1, sl 1] twice, p1, k1, [p1, sl 1] twice, p1 *, k1, p1, sl 1, p1, k5, p1, sl 1, p1, k1, rep between *'s once, k2. **31** K1, p1, sl 1, p1, *[k1, (p1, sl 1) twice, p1] twice *, k3, p1, k2, rep between *'s once, k1, p1, sl 1, p1, k1. **33** Rep row 9. **35** Rep row 31. **37** Rep row 29. **39** Rep row 3. **41** Rep row 13. **43** Rep row 11. **45** Rep row 9. **47** Rep row 19. **49** Rep row 17. **51** Rep row 3. **53** Rep row 13. **55** Rep row 11. **57** Rep row 9. **59** Rep row 7. **61** Rep row 5. **63** Rep row 3. **65** Rep row 1.

☐ K on RS, p on WS
☐ P on RS
☑ Sl 1 purlwise with yarn in front

Chart Pat

64 · 62 · 60 · 58 · 56 · 54 · 52 · 50 · 48 · 46 · 44 · 42 · 40 · 38 · 36 · 34 · 32 · 30 · 28 · 26 · 24 · 22 · 20 · 18 · 16 · 14 · 12 · 10 · 8 · 6 · 4 · 2

65 · 63 · 61 · 59 · 57 · 55 · 53 · 51 · 49 · 47 · 45 · 43 · 41 · 39 · 37 · 35 · 33 · 31 · 29 · 27 · 25 · 23 · 21 · 19 · 17 · 15 · 13 · 11 · 9 · 7 · 5 · 3 · 1

39 sts

Marge Hayes
ABERDEEN, SOUTH DAKOTA

My grandmother taught me to knit, but I've been a serious knitter since the early '70s when I taught myself to knit the continental way.

I'm a very visual person—when the vision for this square came, I caught a glimpse of cables, some sort of openwork, bobbles, and a tendril-y center.

It was only after I started knitting that I realized how all the parts went together—garter stitch represents the running band of a brick wall; smooth stockinette stitch, like patches of lawn bisected by a path; branches, clover, leaves, and finally bobbles that look like raspberries. I didn't know how I would finish the center until I got there and it came to me. I'd use I-cord—perfect for stamens!

Yarn color #2453

10cm/4"
26
18
• over stockinette st
(k on RS, p on WS)

• 4.5mm/US 7, or size to obtain gauge, 60cm/24" long

five • 4.5mm/US 7

&

• cable needle (cn)
• st markers

This square originally appeared in Knitter's K45.

Note
See *School*, page 60, for Make 1 (M1), SSK, SSP, SK2P, and I-cord.

Square
Cast on 196 sts onto circular needle, placing a marker after each set of 49 sts. Join, place marker and work rnds 1–45 of Chart A (change to dpns when necessary)—12 sts.
Regroup sts so there are 4 sts on each of 3 dpns. Draw a length of yarn through sts to use in tightening up later but leave sts on needles. Work 2" of I-cord on each needle, drawing yarn through sts at end. Using photo as guide, loop I-cord over and fasten securely on wrong side.

Leaves Make 4
Cast on 5 sts. Work rows 1–33 of Chart B. Bind off rem 6 sts.

Finishing
Block pieces. Sew on leaves, tacking down tips. Steam gently without flattening.

IN OTHER WORDS
Make bobble (MB) [K1, yo, k1, yo, k1] in one st—5 sts. Turn, k5. Turn, p5. Turn, k5. Turn and pass 2nd, 3rd, 4th and 5th sts, one at a time, over first st. K 1 st.
3/3 RC Sl 3 to cn, hold to back, k3; k3 from cn.
3/3 LC Sl 3 to cn, hold to front, k3; k3 from cn.

Chart A *49-ST REPEAT*
Rnds 1, 3, and 5 Knit. **2** SSP, p45, p2tog—47 sts. **4** SSP, p43, p2tog—45 sts. **6** SSP, p41, p2tog—43 sts. **7** K12, p2, yo, SSK, yo, p2, k2, M1, k3, M1, k2, p2, yo, SSK, yo, p2, k12—47 sts. **8** SSK, k10, p2, k3, p2, k9, p2, k3, p2, k10, k2tog—45 sts. **9** K11, p2, k1, yo, SSK, p2, 3/3 RC, k3, p2, k1, yo, SSK, p2, k11. **10** SSK, [k9, p2, k3, p2] twice, k9, k2tog—43 sts. **11** K10, p2, k3, p2, k9, p2, k3, p2, k10. **12** SSK, k8, p2, k3, p2, k9, p2, k3, p2, k8, k2tog—41 sts. **13** K9, p2, yo, SK2P, yo, p2, k3, 3/3 LC, p2, yo, SK2P, yo, p2, k9. **14** SSK, k7, p2,

k3, p2, k9, p2, k3, p2, k7, k2tog—39 sts. **15** K8, p2, k1, yo, SSK, p2, k9, p2, k1, yo, SSK, p2, k8. **16** SSK, k6, p2, k3, p2, k9, p2, k3, p2, k6, k2tog—37 sts. **17** K7, p2, k3, p2, 3/3 RC, [k3, p2] twice, k7. **18** SSK, k5, p2, k3, p2, k9, p2, k3, p2, k5, k2tog—35 sts. **19** K6, p2, yo, SK2P, yo, p2, k9, p2, yo, SK2P, yo, p2, k6. **20** SSK, k4, p2, k3, p2, k9, p2, k3, p2, k4, k2tog—33 sts. **21** K5, p2, k1, yo, SSK, p2, k3, 3/3 LC, p2, k1, yo, SSK, p2, k5. **22** SSK, [k3, p2] twice, k9, [p2, k3] twice, k2tog—31 sts. **23** K4, p2, k3, p2, k9, p2, k3, p2, k4. **24** SSK, k2, p2, k3, p2, k9, p2, k3, p2, k2, k2tog—29 sts. **25** K3, p2, yo, SK2P, yo, p2, 3/3 RC, k3, p2, yo, SK2P, yo, p2, k3. **26** SSK, k1, p2, k3, p2, k9, p2, k3, p2, k1, k2tog—27 sts. **27** K2, p2, k1, yo, SSK, p2, k9, p2, k1, yo, SSK, p2, k2. **28** SSK, p2, k3, p2, k9, p2, k3, p2, k2tog—25 sts. **29** K1, [p2, k3] twice, 3/3 LC, p2, k3, p2, k1. **30** SSK, p1, k3, p2, k9, p2, k3, p1, k2tog—23 sts. **31** K1, p1, yo, SK2P, yo, p2, k9, p2, yo, SK2P, yo, p1, k1. **32** SSK, k3, p2, k9, p2, k3, k2tog—21 sts. **33** K2, yo, SSK, p2, 3/3 RC, k3, p2, k1, yo, SSK, k1. **34** SSK, k2, p2, k9, p2, k2, k2tog—19 sts. **35** K3, p2, k9, p2, k3. **36** SSK, k1, p2, k9, p2, k1, k2tog—17 sts. **37** K2, p2, k3, 3/3 LC, p2, k2. **38** SSK, p2, k9, p2, k2tog—15 sts. **39** K1, p2, k9, p2, k1. **40** SSK, p1, k9, p1, k2tog—13 sts. **41** SSK, 3/3 RC, k3, k2tog—11 sts. **42** SSK, k1, MB, k3, MB, k1, k2tog—9 sts. **43** SSK, k5, k2tog—7 sts. **44** SSK, k3, k2tog—5 sts. **45** SSK, MB, k2tog—3 sts.

Chart B *BEGIN ON 5 STS*
(**Note** Sl sts purlwise with yarn in back.)
Row 1 (RS) K5. **2** (WS) K5. **3, 5, 7, and 9** K1, M1, k to last st, M1, k1. **4, 6, and 8** Knit. **10** K6, place marker (pm), p1, pm, k6. **11, 13, 15, 17, 19, 21, 23, and 25** K1, M1, k to marker, sl 1, k to last st, M1, k1. **12, 14, 16, 18, 20, 22, 24, 26, and 28** K to marker, p1, k to end. **27** K to marker, sl 1, k to end. **29 and 31** K2, SSK, k to 2 sts before marker, SSK, sl 1, k2tog, k to last 4 sts, k2tog, k2. **30 and 32** K3, k2tog, k to 2 sts before marker, k2tog, p1, SSK, k to last 5 sts, SSK, k3. **33** [SSK] 3 times, SK2P, [k2tog] twice—6 sts.

Chart B

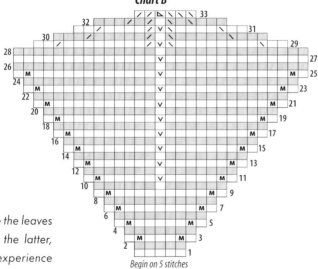

Begin on 5 stitches

Legend:

- ☐ K on RS, p on WS
- ▨ P on RS, k on WS
- ╱ K2tog on RS
- ╲ SSK on RS
- ▞ P2tog on RS, k2tog on WS
- ▚ SSP on RS, SSK on WS
- **M** Make 1
- **O** Yarn over (yo)
- **B** Make bobble (MB)
- ◣ SK2P
- **V** Sl 1 purlwise with yarn in back
- ⧓ 3/3 RC
- ⧓ 3/3 LC

Editor's Note

You either really love the leaves or you really don't. If the latter, make just one to experience their simple and very effective shaping. The square is beautiful without leaves.

Chart A

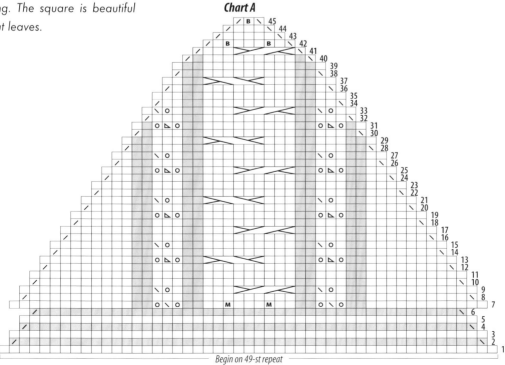

Begin on 49-st repeat

39

Julie Hoff-Weisenberger

WHEELING, WEST VIRGINIA

I learned to knit while living in Salzburg, Austria during college. I came back to the United States not knowing any knitting terms in English, so I pretty much taught myself by trial and error. For a few years after college, I designed machine knits. I now design exclusively for hand-knitting and I especially enjoy creating original stitch patterns such as twining oak leaf and acorn.

Note

See *School*, page 60, for Make 1 (M1), SSK, SK2P S2KP2, knit into front and back (kf&b), and purl into front and back (pf&b).

Square

Cast on 56 sts. K 6 rows, inc 8 sts evenly across on last (RS) row—64 sts. ***Beg Chart Pat: Row 1*** (WS) K3, work chart pat over 28 sts, p2, work chart pat over 28 sts, k3. ***2*** K3, work chart pat over 26 sts, k2, work chart pat over 26 sts, k3. Keeping first and last 3 sts in garter st, cont in pat as established over center sts through chart row 48, then rep rows 1–24 once more—64 sts. K 5 rows, dec 8 sts on first row—56 sts. Bind off.

IN OTHER WORDS

5/3 LPC Dec Sl 5 to cn, hold to front, p3; from cn SSK, k1, k2tog; turn; p3; turn, SK2P.
5/3 RPC Dec Sl 3 to cn, hold to back, SSK, k1, k2tog; turn; p3; turn; k3tog; p3 from cn.

Chart pat *BEGIN ON 28 STS*

Row 1 (WS) K2, k2tog, k2, p5, k2, k2tog, k1, p3, k9—26 sts. ***2*** P7, p2tog, kf&b, k2, p4, k2, M1, k1, M1, k2, p5—28 sts. ***3*** K5, p7, k4, p2, k1, p1, k8. ***4*** P6, p2tog, k1, pf&b, k2, p4, SSK, k3, k2tog, p5—26 sts. ***5*** K5, p5, k4, p2, k2, p1, k7. ***6*** P5, p2tog, k1, p1, pf&b, k2, p4, SSK, k1, k2tog, p5—24 sts. ***7*** K5, p3, k4, p2, k3, p1, k6. ***8*** P4, p2tog, k1, p2, pf&b, k1, M1, k1, p2tog, p2, S2KP2, p5—22 sts. ***9*** K9, p3, k4, p1, k5. ***10*** P5, [(k1, yo) 3 times, k1] in next st, p4, k1, kf&b, k1, p2tog, p7—28 sts. ***11*** K8, p1, k1, p2, k4, p7, k5. ***12*** P5, k3, M1, k1, M1, k3, p4, k2, pf&b, k1, p2tog, p6—30 sts. ***13*** K7, p1, k2, p2, k4, p9, k5. ***14*** P5, k4, M1, k1, M1, k4, p4, k2, p2, [(k1, yo) twice, k1] in next st, p7—36 sts. ***15*** K14, p2, k4, p11, k5. ***16*** P5, [k1, M1] twice, [k3, M1, k1, M1] twice, k1, p4, k2, p2, k5, p7—42 sts. ***17*** K14, p2, k4, p17, k5. ***18*** P2, 5/3 RPC Dec, k7, 5/3 LPC Dec, p1, k2, p2, k5, p7—34 sts. ***19*** K7, p5, k2, p2, k1, k2tog, k2, p7, k2, k2tog, k2—32 sts. ***20*** P5, k3, M1, k1, M1, k3, p4, k2, p2, k5, p7—34 sts. ***21*** K7, p5, k2, p2, k4, p9, k5. ***22*** P5, [(k1, M1) twice, k1] 3 times, p4, k2, p2, k5, p7—40 sts. ***23*** K7, p5, k2, p2, k4, p15, k5. ***24*** P2, 5/3 RPC Dec, k5, 5/3 LPC Dec, p1, k1, M1, k1, p2, k5tog, p2tog, p5—28 sts. ***25*** K9, p3, k1, k2tog, k2, p5, k2, k2tog, k2—26 sts. ***26*** P5, k2, M1, k1, M1, k2, p4, k1, kf&b, k1, p2tog, p7—28 sts. ***27*** K8, p1, k1, p2, k4, p7, k5. ***28*** P5, SSK, k3, k2tog, p4, k2, pf&b, k1, p2tog, p6—26 sts. ***29*** K7, p1, k2, p2, k4, p5, k5. ***30*** P5, SSK, k1, k2tog, p4, k2, pf&b, p1, k1, p2tog, p5—24 sts. ***31*** K6, p1, k3, p2, k4, p3, k5. ***32*** P5, S2KP2, p2, p2tog, k1, M1, k1, pf&b, p2, k1, p2tog, p4—22 sts. ***33*** K5, p1, k4, p3, k9. ***34*** P7, p2tog, kf&b, k2, p4, [(k1, yo) 3 times, k1] in next st, p5—28 sts. ***35*** K5, p7, k4, p2, k1, p1, k8. ***36*** P6, p2tog, k1, pf&b, k2, p4, k3, M1, k1, M1, k3, p5—30 sts. ***37*** K5, p9, k4, p2, k2, p1, k7. ***38*** P7, [(k1, yo) twice, k1] in next st, p2, k2, p4, k4, M1, k1, M1, k4, p5—36 sts. ***39*** K5, p11, k4, p2, k14. ***40*** P7, k5, p2, k2, p4, [k1, M1] twice, [k3, M1, k1, M1] twice, k1, p5—42 sts. ***41*** K5, p17, k4, p2, k14. ***42*** P7, k5, p2, k2, p1, 5/3 RPC Dec, k7, 5/3 LPC Dec, p2—34 sts. ***43*** K2, k2tog, k2, p7, k2, k2tog, k1, p2, k2, p5, k7—32 sts. ***44*** P7, k5, p2, k2, p4, k3, M1, k1, M1, k3, p5—34 sts. ***45*** K5, p9, k4, p2, k2, p5, k7. ***46*** P7, k5, p2, k2, p4, [(k1, M1) twice, k1] 3 times, p5—40 sts. ***47*** K5, p15, k4, p2, k2, p5, k7. ***48*** P5, p2tog, k5tog, p2, k1, M1, k1, p1, 5/3 RPC Dec, k5, 5/3 LPC Dec, p2—28 sts.

Yarn color #9445

10cm/4"
28

20
• **over stockinette st**
(k on RS, p on WS)

• 4.5mm/US 7, or size to obtain gauge

&

• cable needle (cn)

This square originally appeared in Knitter's K44.

□ K on RS, p on WS
▨ P on RS, k on WS
■ Sts do not exist in
   these areas of chart
╱ K2tog on RS
╲ SSK
╱ P2tog on RS, k2tog on WS
▲ S2KP2
△ K5 tog
M Make 1 (M1)
Y K into front and back of st (kf&b)
Y P into front and back of st (pf&b)
7 [(K1, yo) 3 times, k1] in a st
5 [(K1, yo) twice, k1] in a st
▬▬ 5/3 LPC Dec
▬▬ 5/3 RPC Dec

Chart Pat

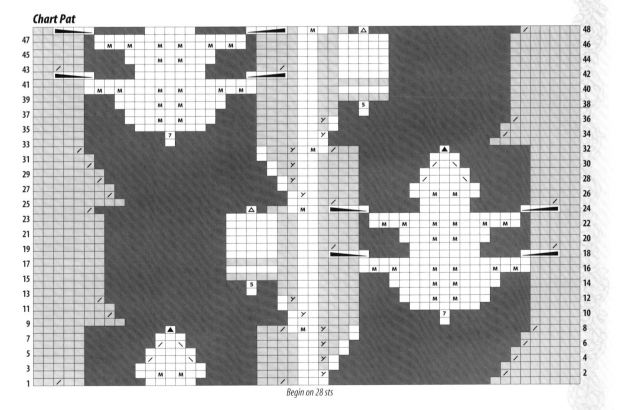

Begin on 28 sts

Karen Kendrick-Hands

GROSSE POINTE PARK, MICHIGAN

I have always wanted to knit, even though there were no knitters in my family. Finally when I was 12, I learned that my neighbor, a cook in the school cafeteria, knit and would teach me.

This square pleases me as it has a little bit of entrelac with knit and purl textures, a little lace, and a little cable. I began with a spiral built from twelve 6-stitch rectangles. I used texture to emphasize the middle ring. Adapting the round peg to fill a square hole was a challenge, as was filling the center with a spiral rosette with stitches picked up from the edge of the hole and worked inward. Imagine my joy when I realized I could increase with yarn-overs to create a little lace, and make the central stitch at each corner a 3-stitch braid.

Yarn color #9489

10cm/4"

28

20

• *over stockinette stitch (k on RS, p on WS)*

five 4mm/US 6, or size to obtain gauge

• 4mm/US 6, 40cm/16" and 60cm/24" long

&

• cable needle (cn)
• stitch markers

This square originally appeared in Knitter's K44.

Notes

1 See *School*, page 60, for SSK, SK2P, Make 1 (M1) and yo before a k and p st. **2** When working rectangles, sl first st of each row purlwise. On RS rows, sl st with yarn in back; on WS rows, sl st with yarn in front. **3** Turn work after every row of rectangles, unless otherwise instructed. **4** Change to longer circular needle when necessary.

1/1 LC Sl 1 to cn, hold to front, k1; k1 from cn.
1/2 RC Sl 2 to cn, hold to back, k1; k2 from cn.

Square
Inner ring
First rectangle
With 16" circular needle, cast on 6 sts, leaving an 8" tail. Beg with a k row, work in St st for 11 rows—1 rectangle completed.

Next rectangle
*With RS facing and dpn, pick up and k 5 sts along chain st selvage at left edge of rectangle as foll: skip first st, then pick up and k 1 st in each of the next 5 sts. **Next row** (WS) Sl 1, p4. **Next row** Sl 1, M1, k4—6 sts. Beg with a p row, work in St st for 10 rows, working last row with right needle of circular needle—rectangle completed. Rep from* 10 times more—12 rectangles. With cast-on tail, seam cast-on edge of first rectangle to side of last rectangle to close ring.

Middle ring
*With RS facing, pick up and k 6 sts along right edge of next rectangle from inner ring. **Rows 1 and 3** (WS) Sl 1, p5. **Row 2** Sl 1, [p1, k1] twice, SSK last st with next st on left needle. **Row 4** Sl 1, [k1, p1] twice, SSK with next st on left needle. Rep rows 1–4 twice more. Do not turn after last row has been worked. Rep from* 11 times more—12 rectangles.

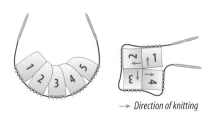

→ *Direction of knitting*

A. Inner Ring
Work Rectangles 1–12, always picking up on left side of previous rectangle.

B.
Seam cast-on edge of Rectangle 1 to left edge of 12.

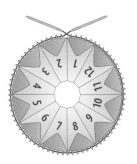

D. Outer Ring
Pick up 6 sts and knit 6 sts from each block.

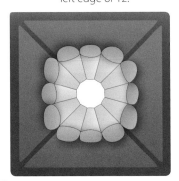

E.
Place double increases at 4 corners to form square.

Outer ring

Work in rnds as foll: Place marker (pm) for beg of rnd. **Rnd 1** With circular needle, [pick up and k 6 sts along right edge of next rectangle from middle ring, then k6 from needle] 12 times—144 sts. **Rnd 2** [(K2tog) 3 times, k6] 12 times—108 sts. **Rnd 3** (**Note** The 8 corner markers should be a different color from rnd marker.) K7, [yo, pm, k3, pm, yo, k24] 3 times, yo, pm, k3, pm, yo, k17—116 sts. **Rnd 4** K8, [sl corner marker (sm), 1/2 RC, sm, k26] 3 times, sm, 1/2 RC, sm, k18. **Rnd 5** K8, [yo, sm, k3, sm, yo, k26] 3 times, yo, sm, k3, sm, yo, k18—124 sts. **Rnd 6** K9, [sm, k1, 1/1 LC, sm, k28] 3 times, sm, k1, 1/1 LC, sm, k19. **Rnds 7–19** Cont to work 3 sts between each pair of corner markers in cable pat as established, and work all incs into St st—180 sts (40 sts between yo's in each St st section). **Rnd 20** K16, [1/2 RC, k42] 3 times, 1/2 RC, k21. Reposition rnd marker at this point for beg of rnd 21. Remove corner markers.

Garter border

Rnd 21 P21, [yo, k3, yo, p42] 3 times, yo, k3, yo, p21—188 sts. **Rnd 22** K22, [yo, SK2P, yo, k44] 3 times, yo, SK2P, yo, k22. **Rnd 23** P23, [yo, p1, yo, p46] 3 times, yo, p1, yo, p23—196 sts. **Rnd 24** Knit. **Rnd 25** P24, [yo, p1, yo, p48] 3 times, yo, p1, yo, p24—204 sts. **Rnd 26** Knit. Bind off.

Center rosette

With RS facing and dpns, pick up and k 35 sts along selvage of inner ring. Divide sts over 4 needles. **Rnd 1** Knit. **2** [K3, k2tog] 7 times. **3** [K2, k2tog] 7 times. **4** [K1, k2tog] 7 times. **5** [K2tog] 7 times. Cut yarn, draw through rem 7 sts and tighten.

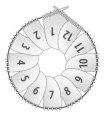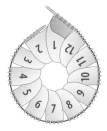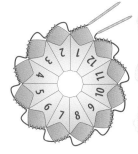

C. Middle Ring

Pick up 6 stitches along edge of 1... ...and work a rectangle with SSK decreases along stitches from 1. Repeat for other rectangles.

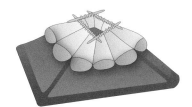

F. Center Rosette

Pick up 35 stitches from center hole and work decrease rounds.

Joan Schrouder
EUGENE, OREGON

I learned the rudiments of knitting at age 8 from a classmate, but as no one in my immediate family knit, I was on my own. I had to figure out the details by myself, which was an invaluable experience.

By the time I was an adult and started reading how-to books, I was confident enough not to be swayed by the "must-ought-shoulds." In fact, I must admit to taking perverse pleasure in proving an axiom wrong!

The concept for this square was created by just such a warped rationalization. If I wanted a conventional square with the corners radiating out in nearly straight lines from the center point, I'd have to increase on one side of the corner points on the odd rounds, then on the other side on the even rounds. "But what if the increases were kept only on the same side?" I mused. Here you see the results: my twirly, whirly, swirly, squirrely square!

Yarn color #2440

10cm/4"

26 **18**

• **over stockinette stitch (k on RS, p on WS)**

• Five 5mm/US 8, or size to obtain gauge

• 5mm/US 8, 60cm/24" long

&

• St markers

This square originally appeared in Knitter's K42.

Notes
1 See *School*, page 60, for Make 1 knit (M1K) and purl (M1P). **2** Change to circular needle when necessary, placing a marker between sts from each needle to mark 4 sections.

Square
Cast on 8 sts. Distribute them evenly among 4 dpns. Join.
Rnd 1 Knit.
Rnd 2 [K2, M1K] 4 times—12 sts.
Rnd 3 [K3, M1K] 4 times—16 sts.
Rnd 4 [K4, M1K] 4 times—20 sts.
Rnd 5 [K5, M1K] 4 times—24 sts.
Rnd 6 [K6, M1K] 4 times—28 sts.
Rnd 7 [P7, M1P] 4 times—32 sts.
Rnd 8 [P8, M1P] 4 times—36 sts.

Rnd 9 [P9, M1P] 4 times—40 sts.
Rnd 10 [P10, M1P] 4 times—44 sts.
Rnd 11 [P11, M1P] 4 times—48 sts.
Rnd 12 [P12, M1P] 4 times—52 sts.
Rnds 13–48 Cont to alternate 6 rnds of knit with 6 rnds of purl, inc 1 st at end of each needle, until there are 4 bands each of knit and purl—49 sts in each section.
Garter border
Mark 4 inc sts as corner sts.
***Next rnd** Knit.
Next rnd Purl, working (M1P, k1, M1P) at each corner. Rep from* twice more—55 sts in each section. Bind off.

Barbara Venishnick

SIMSBURY, CONNECTICUT

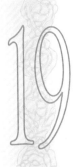

I learned to knit at five years old. My mother taught me with yarn she ripped from a sweater she had started for me. At the age of nine I finished my first sweater, made with yarn we bought together on the Lower East Side of Manhattan. Knitting has been my love ever since.

After a good deal of thought, I realized that entrelac was the stitch I most enjoyed working with. Then it was just a matter of what form it should take. Well, we had to use garter stitch at the border, why not carry it through the whole square. How about breaking it up with a small cable? Thus, after a few false starts, my garter and cable interlace was born.

Yarn colors
MC #9408
CC #9488

10cm/4"
34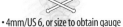
18
• over garter stitch (k every row)

• 4mm/US 6, or size to obtain gauge

&
• cable needle (cn)
• stitch holders

This square originally appeared in Knitter's K43.

Note
See *School*, page 60, for Make 1 knit (M1K) and purl (M1P).

Square
With MC, cast on 56 sts. K 5 rows, dec 2 sts on last row—54 sts. **Next row** (RS) K3 and place these 3 sts on hold, [k1, k2tog] 16 times, place rem 3 sts on hold. Cut MC.
Work center 32 sts as foll:
Next row (WS) Join CC and p32.

BEG ENTRELAC PAT
(**Notes 1** Turn work after every row, unless otherwise indicated. **2** Cut yarn after every tier of triangles or rectangles has been completed.)
Tier 1: Make 4 Base Triangles with CC
Row 1 (RS) K2.
Row 2 (WS) K2.
Rows 3 and 4 K3.
Rows 5 and 6 K4.
Rows 7 and 8 K5.
Rows 9 and 10 K6.
Rows 11 and 12 K7.
Row 13 K8. Do not turn. [Rep rows 1–13 on next 8 sts] 3 times. Turn work after last triangle has been worked.
Tier 2: Make 1 Left Side Triangle with MC
Row 1 (WS) K2.
Row 2 (RS) K2.
Row 3 K1, M1K, k2tog (1 CC st tog with 1 MC st).
Row 4 K3.

Row 5 K1, M1K, k1, k2tog.
Row 6 K4.
Row 7 K1, M1K, k2, k2tog.
Row 8 K5.
Row 9 K1, M1K, k3, k2tog.
Row 10 K6.
Row 11 K1, M1K, k4, k2tog.
Row 12 K7.
Row 13 K1, M1K, k5, k2tog. Do not turn.
Make 3 Garter Rectangles with MC
With WS facing, pick up and p8 sts along side edge of first base triangle (or cable rectangle).
Row 1 (RS) K8.
Row 2 K7, k2tog (1 CC st tog with 1 MC st).
Rows 3–16 Rep rows 1 and 2 seven times more. Do not turn. Work 2 more rectangles in same way.
Make 1 Right Side Triangle with MC
With WS facing, pick up and p8 sts along outside edge of final base triangle (or cable rectangle).
Row 1 (RS) K8.
Row 2 (WS) K8.
Row 3 K2tog, k6.
Row 4 K7.
Row 5 K2tog, k5.
Row 6 K6.
Row 7 K2tog, k4.
Row 8 K5.
Row 9 K2tog, k3.
Row 10 K4.
Row 11 K2tog, k2.

Tier 1

Make 4 Base Triangles with CC.

Tier 2

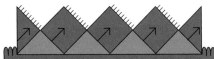

Make 1 Left Side Triangle, 3 Garter Rectangles, and 1 Right Side Triangle with MC.

Row 12 K3.

Row 13 K2tog, k1.

Row 14 K2.

Tier 3: Make 4 Cable Rectangles with CC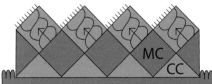

With RS facing, k2tog (sts from right side triangle), then pick up and k7 sts along edge of triangle—8 sts.

Row 1 (WS) K1, p6, k1.

Row 2 (RS) P1, k6, p2tog (1 MC st tog with 1 CC st).

Rows 3 and 4 Rep rows 1 and 2.

Row 5 Rep row 1.

Row 6 P1, sl 3 sts to cn, hold to back, k3; k3 from cn, p2tog.

Rows 7–10 Rep rows 1 and 2 twice.

Row 11 Rep row 1.

Row 12 Rep row 6.

Rows 13–16 Rep rows 1 and 2 twice. Do not turn work after last row.

[With RS facing, pick up and k8 sts along side of next MC rectangle, rep rows 1-16] 3 times. Turn work.

Rep Tiers 2 and 3 twice more, then rep Tier 2 once.

Tier 4: Make 4 Top Triangles with CC

With RS facing, k2tog, then pick up and k7 sts along edge of triangle—8 sts.

Row 1 (WS) K7, turn, leaving 1 st on left needle unworked.

Row 2 (RS) K6, k2tog.

Row 3 K6, turn, leaving 2 sts.

Row 4 K5, k2tog.

Row 5 K5, turn, leaving 3 sts.

Row 6 K4, k2tog.

Row 7 K4, turn, leaving 4 sts.

Row 8 K3, k2tog.

Row 9 K3, turn, leaving 5 sts.

Row 10 K2, k2tog.

Row 11 K2, turn, leaving 6 sts.

Row 12 K1, k2tog.

Row 13 K1, turn, leaving 7 sts.

Row 14 K3tog. Do not turn.

[With RS facing, pick up and k8 sts along edge of next MC rectangle, rep rows 1-14] 3 times. Turn work after last triangle.

Next row (WS) With CC, work across all 32 sts as foll: P1, M1P, [p2, M1P] 15 times, p1—48 sts. Place sts on hold. Cut yarn. Return to 3 sts on holders at each side. Rejoin MC at inside edge (ready to work a RS row on left side and a WS row on right side) and k every row until strip fits along side of square when slightly stretched, end with a WS row. Cut yarn on left side strip only. Place all 54 sts on needle, ready to work a RS row.

Next row (RS) Knit, inc 2 sts—56 sts. K 5 rows more. Bind off. Sew side strips to square.

Tier 4

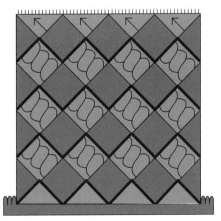

Make 4 Top Edge Triangles with CC.

Tier 3

Make 4 Cable Rectangles with CC.
Repeat Tiers 2 and 3 twice more.
Then repeat Tier 2 once more.

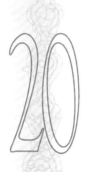

Diane Zangl

LOMIRA, WISCONSIN

I like to adapt common needlework techniques to knitting methods. This square, influenced by French knot and lazy daisy embroidery stitches, is created by reaching down and pulling up stitches to create the "leaves" while the "buds" are a small bobble. The leaves and buds could also be worked in colors.

I've been sewing, embroidering, and crocheting since I was seven, and knitting for over 25 years. I think I inherited my knitting skills from my Italian fraternal grandmother who came to America as a young wife with three small children. Although she couldn't speak English, she could look at a picture and duplicate it perfectly.

Yarn color #2452

10cm/4"

21

17

• over stockinette stitch
(k on RS, p on WS)

• 5mm/US 8, or size to obtain gauge

This square originally appeared in Knitter's K43.

Bud St
[K1, yo, k1] in next st. Turn, p3. Turn, sl 3 sts to RH needle, pass 2nd, then 3rd st over first st.

Square
Cast on 56 sts. K 5 rows, dec 3 sts evenly on last (WS) row—53 sts.
Beg Flower Pat: Rows 1, 3 and 5 (RS) Knit.
Row 2 and all WS rows K3, p47, k3.
Row 7 K5, [work 3-st Flower Leaves, k7] 4 times, work 3-st Flower Leaves, k5.
Row 9 K6, [work Bud St, k9] 4 times, work Bud St, k6.

Rows 11, 13, and 15 Knit.
Row 17 K10, [work 3-st Flower Leaves, k7] 4 times, k3.
Row 19 K11, [work Bud St, k9] 4 times, k2.
Row 20 Rep row 2.
Rep rows 1–20 twice more, then work rows 1–4 once more. K 6 rows, inc 3 sts evenly on first row—56 sts. Bind off.

3-St Flower Leaves The flower leaves are worked over 3 stitches. The Right Leaf is worked between Stitches 1 and 2, and the Left Leaf is worked between Stitches 2 and 3.

Right Leaf

1

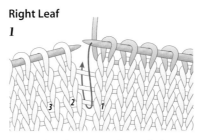

Knit Stitch 1, then insert right needle between Stitches 1 and 2 three rows below, as shown.

2

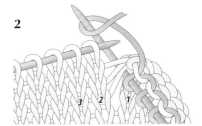

Wrap yarn knitwise around right needle.

Left Leaf

6

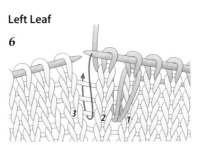

Knit Stitch 2, then insert right needle between Stitches 2 and 3 three rows below.

7

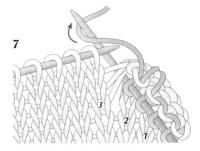

Wrap yarn clockwise around needle, pull up a long stitch.

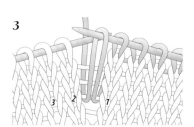

3

Pull up a long, loose stitch.

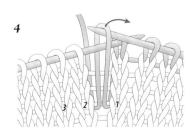

4

Slip long stitch and Stitch 1 to left needle, then pass long stitch over Stitch 1.

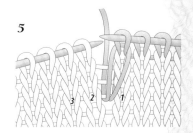

5

Slip Stitch 1 back to right needle.

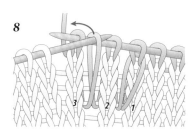

8

Knit Stitch 3, then pass long stitch over Stitch 3.

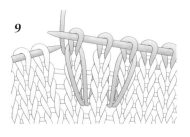

9

3-stitch flower leaves completed.

Sally Melville
WATERLOO, ONTARIO, CANADA

I remember knitting very young and beginning to "design" as a teenager—not from any need to be creative but simply because I couldn't match gauge. Fortunately, there was no one around to just tell me to use smaller needles—that was an early learning experience of the ever-present silver lining.

Once, as a parent chaperone, I found myself faced with long hours on a bus. I knew, for simplicity's sake, I should probably take only one color of yarn. I decided to try for a garment with many and constant changes in stitch pattern.

One very tattered sketch and many bus hours later, I had produced a sweater that used approximately two dozen stitch patterns, including lace, bobbles, cables, and knit and purl patterns. This afghan piece is a small section of that garment.

Yarn color #2452

10cm/4"
26
18½
• over stockinette stitch
(k on RS, p on WS)

• 4.5mm/US 7, or size to obtain gauge

&

• cable needle (cn)

This square originally appeared in Knitter's K44.

Notes
1 See *School*, page 60, for knit cast-on, Make 1 knit or purl (M1K or M1P), knit or purl into front and back of st (kf&b or pf&b), SSK, and SK2P. *2* Slip sts purlwise with yarn at WS of work.

Square
Cast on 55 sts. Knit 5 rows. **Beg Chart Pat: Row 1** (RS) K3, work chart pat over 49 sts, k3. Keeping first and last 3 sts in garter st, cont working chart pat over center sts, through chart row 80. K 6 rows. Bind off.

IN OTHER WORDS
Make bobble (MB) K into [front and back of next st] twice; turn, p4; turn, k4; turn, p4; turn, sl1-k3tog-psso.
1/1 RC Sl 1 to cn, hold to back, k1; k1 from cn.
1/1 RPC Sl 1 to cn, hold to back, k1; p1 from cn.
1/1 LPC Sl 1 to cn, hold to front, p1; k1 from cn.
Cast-on Bobble (MCB) Knit cast on 3 sts; p4; pass 2nd, 3rd, 4th sts over first—1 st rem.
M2P P into front and back of horizontal bar between sts.
2/1 LPC Sl 2 sts to cn, hold to front, p1; k2 from cn.
3/1 LC Sl 3 to cn, hold to front, k1; k3 from cn.
3/1 LPC Sl 3 to cn, hold to front, p1; k3 from cn.
4/1 LPC Sl 4 to cn, hold to front, p1; k4 from cn.
4/1 LIC Sl 4 to cn, hold to front, k in front and back of next st; k4 from cn.

Chart pat
Row 1 (RS) Knit. *2* P1, k into front and back of st (kf&b), [p1, k6, p1, k7] twice, p1, k3, p4, k1, p4, k3, p1. *3* K1, p3, k2, kf&b, k1, p into front and back of st (pf&b), k1, kf&b, k2, p3, k1, [p6, 1/1 RC, p5, 1/1 RC] twice, p2, k1. *4* P1, k2, [p2, k5, p2, k6] twice, p1, k3, p5, k2, p5,
k3, p1. *5* K1, p3, k5, p2, k5, p3, k1, [p5, 1/1 RPC, k1, p3, k1, 1/1 RC, k1] twice, p2, k1. *6* P1, k2, [p4, k3, p1, k1, p1, k5] twice, p1, k3, p5, k2, p5, k3, p1. *7* K1, p2, pf&b, k4, SSK, k2tog, k4, pf&b, p2, k1, [p4, 1/1 RPC, p1, k2, p2, (k1, M1) twice, k2] twice, p2, k1. *8* P1, k2, [p6, k2, p2, k2, p1, k4] twice, p1, k4, p10, k4, p1. *9* K1, p3, 1/1 RPC, 4/1 LPC, k2tog, k2, pf&b, p3, k1, [p4, k1, p2, k1, 1/1 LPC, p1, k2, (M1, k1) twice, k2] twice, p2, k1. *10* P1, [k2, p8, (k1, p1) twice, k2, p1, k2] twice, k2, p1, k5, p7, k2, p1, k3, p1. *11* K1, p2, 1/1 RPC, p2, 4/1 LPC, k2tog, pf&b, p4, k1, [p4, k1, p2, (k1, p1) twice, k8] twice, p2, k1. *12* P1, k2, [p8, (k1, p1) twice, k2, p1, k4] twice, p1, k6, p5, k4, p1, k2, p1. *13* K1, p1, 1/1 RPC, p3, 1/1 RPC, 3/1 LPC, p6, k1, [p4, k1, p2, (k1, p1) twice, SSK, k3, k2tog, k1] twice, p2, k1. *14* P1, k2, [p6, (k1, p1) twice, k2, p1, k4] twice, p1, k6, p3, k2, p1, k4, p1, k1, p1. *15* K1, p1, 1/1 LPC, p2, 1/1 RPC, p2, 3/1 LPC, p5, k1, [p3, MCB, k1, MCB, (p1, k1) twice, p1, SSK, k1, k2tog, M1P, k1] twice, p2, k1. *16* P1, k2, p1, k1, *p3, [k1, p1] twice, k1, sl 1, p1, sl 1, k3* p1, k1, rep between *'s once, p1, k5, p3, k4, [p1, k2] twice, p1. *17* K1, p2, 1/1 LPC, 1/1 RPC, p3, 1/1 RPC, 2/1 LPC, p4, *k1, p1, [p1, MCB] 3 times, [k1, MCB] twice, SK2P, M1P, p1; rep from* once, k1, p2, k1. *18* [P1, k2] twice, [p1, sl 1] 3 times, [k1, sl 1] twice, [k2, p1] twice, [sl 1, p1] twice, [sl 1, k1] 3 times, k1, p1, k4, p2, k2, p1, k4, p2, k3, p1. *19* K1, p3, 2/1 LPC, p2, 1/1 RPC, p2, 2/1 LPC, p3, k1, [p3, (MCB, p1) 5 times, p1, k1] twice, p2tog, k1. *20* [P1, k1] twice, [k1, sl 1] 5 times, k3, p1, k1, [k1, sl 1] 5 times, [k3, p1] twice, p1, k4, p1, k2, p2, k4, p1. *21* K1, p4, 2/1 LPC, 1/1 RPC, p3, 1/1 RPC, 1/1 LPC, p2, k1, [p6, (MCB, p1) twice, p4, k1] twice, p1, k1. *22* P1, k1, [p1, k5, (sl 1,

k1) twice, k5] twice, [p1, k2] 3 times, k2, p3, k5, p1. **23** K1, p5, 3/1 LPC, p2, 1/1 RPC, p2, 1/1 LPC, p1, k33. **24** P1, k31, [p1, k1] twice, k3, p1, k2, p3, k6, p1. **25** K1, p6, 3/1 LPC, 1/1 RPC, p3, 1/1 RPC, p1, k11, yo, SSK, k20. **26** P1, k1, p2, k3, p2, k2, p1, k5, p8, k7, p1, k2, p1, k4, p4, k7, p1. **27** K1, p4, p2tog, k1, 4/1 LIC, p2, 1/1 RPC, p2, k1, p7, k1, k2tog, yo, k1, yo, SSK, k2, p5, k12. **28** P1, k2, p2, k3, p2, k1, p1, k5, p8, k7, p1, k3, p1, k2, p7, k5, p1. **29** K1, p3, p2tog, k3, 4/1 LIC, 1/1 RPC, p3, k1, p7, k2tog, yo, k3, yo, SSK, k1, p2, MB, p2, k12. **30** P1, k3, p2, k3, p3, k2, sl 1, k2, p8, k7, p1, k4, p10, k4, p1. **31** K1, p2, p2tog, k5, M2P, k5, p2tog, p2, k1, p7, k2, yo, SK2P, yo, k3, p5, k12. **32** [P2, k3] 3 times, k2, p8, k7, p1, k3, p5, k2, p5, k3, p1. **33** K1, p3, k5, p2, k5, p3, k1, p7, k3, yo, SSK, k3, p5, k12. **34** P3, k3, p2, k3, p1, k5, p8, k7, p1, k3, p5, k2, p5, k3, p1. **35** K1, p2, pf&b, k4, SSK, k2tog, k4, pf&b, p2, k4, yo, SSK, k2, p7, k1, p5, k12. **36** P1, k1, p2, k3, p2, k2, p1, k5, p1, k7, p8, k4, p10, k4, p1. **37** K1, p3, 1/1 RPC, 4/1 LPC, k2tog, k2, pf&b,

p3, k2, k2tog, yo, k1, yo, SSK, k1, p7, k1, p2, MB, p2, k12. **38** P1, k2, p2, k3, p2, k1, p1, k2, sl 1, k2, p1, k7, p8, k5, p7, k2, p1, k3, p1. **39** K1, p2, 1/1 RPC, p2, 4/1 LPC, k2tog, pf&b, p4, k1, k2tog, yo, k3, yo, SSK, p7, k1, p5, k12. **40** P1, k3, p2, k3, p3, k5, p1, k7, p8, k6, p5, k4, p1, k2, p1. **41** K1, p1, 1/1 RPC, p3, 1/1 RPC, 3/1 LPC, p6, k3, yo, SK2P, yo, k2, p7, k1, p5, k12. **42** [P2, k3] 3 times, k2, p1, k7, p8, k6, p3, k2, p1, k4, p1, k1, p1. **43** K1, p1, 1/1 RPC, p2, 1/1 RPC, p2, 3/1LPC, p5, k4, yo, SSK, k2, p7, k1, p5, k12. (*Continued on page 63*)

(*Continued on page 63*)

Chart found on pages 32–33

Heather Lodinsky
BUFFALO, NEW YORK

I learned to knit from my mother when I was 7 years old. I became an avid knitter in college when I did not have enough room in my dorm room for a sewing machine but plenty of room for yarn and needles! During my graduate school days, I worked in a yarn shop in College Park, Maryland and developed my knitting skills and desire to design.

This square is my attempt to be playful with the knit stitch by showing how it can mimic itself on a large scale.

Since I love the look of stockinette, I wondered if I could come up with a cable that looks like stockinette stitch fabric and this is my result. I also wanted to mimic a cast-on and bind-off edge on a big scale. I found I-cord worked in chain stitch did the trick.

Yarn color #2453

10cm/4"
24
22
• over Chart Pat

• 5mm/US 8, or size to obtain gauge

• two 5mm/US 8

&

• cable needle (cn)
• tapestry needle

This square originally appeared in Knitter's K44.

Note
See *School*, page 60, for I-cord, Make 1 purl (M1P), and SSK.

Square
Cast on 56 sts. K 5 rows, dec 4 sts evenly across on last (WS) row—52 sts. *****Next row** (RS) Knit. **Next row** K3, p to last 3 sts, k3. Rep from * once more. **Next row** (RS) K3, k center 46 sts, inc 20 sts evenly across (to 66 sts), k3—72 sts total. **Beg Chart Pat: Row 1** (WS) K3, work in chart pat to last 3 sts, k3. Keeping 3 sts each side in garter st and center 66 sts in chart pat, work until piece measures 10½" from beg, end with chart row 6. K 5 rows, dec 16 sts evenly across on first row—56 sts. Bind off.

Finishing
Make I-cord trim for both "cast-on" and "bound-off" edges as foll: Using dpns and leaving a 6" tail, cast on 3 sts. Work I-cord for 40". Bind off, leaving a 6" tail. Thread tapestry needle with tail yarn from bound-off end of I-cord. Beg at left side of square (in space between garter st and chart pat), bring up I-cord from back and, using photo as guide, make 7 "stitches." Bring I-cord through last st made. Secure ends.

IN OTHER WORDS
2/2 LPC Sl 2 to cn, hold to front, p2; k2 from cn.
2/2 RPC Sl 2 to cn, hold to back, k2; p2 from cn.

Chart Pat *MULTIPLE OF 9 STS, PLUS 3*
Row 1 (WS) K2, *p3, k2, p3, k1; rep from*, end k1. **2** P1, *p1, 2/2 LPC, 2/2 RPC; rep from*, end p2. **3** K2, *p1, k1, p4, k1, p1, k1; rep from*, end k1. **4** P1, *p1, k2, M1P, SSK, k2tog, M1P, k2; rep from*, end p2. **5** Rep row 1. **6** P1, *p1, k3, p2, k3; rep from*, end p2. Rep rows 1–6 for Chart Pat.

☐ K on RS, p on WS
▨ P on RS, k on WS
Ⓜ M1P
↘ SSK
↗ K2tog
⤬ 2/2 LPC
⤬ 2/2 RPC

Chart Pat

└── 9-st repeat ──┘

Meg Swansen
PITTSVILLE, WISCONSIN

Being a circular knitter by choice, many people assume that I do not like flat or intarsia knitting—an erroneous assumption. I may not like to execute flat or intarsia knitting, but I most certainly have an appreciation for the beauty that may be achieved.

My afghan square is a perverse desire to demonstrate a contradiction: a bit of intarsia that can only be achieved by working in the round. Four contrasting-colored stripes are worked in I-cord. To knit I-cord, the working wool must be coming from the last stitch—an automatic circumstance if attempting circular intarsia. Credit for the concept goes to Kathy Lynch. I installed it at the corners radiating from the center and put an antic knot in each ray. The rays may each be worked in a different color.

Yarn colors
MC #2435
CC #2452

10cm/4"
29
18
• *over stockinette stitch*
(k on RS, p on WS)

five 5mm/US 8, or size to obtain gauge

• 5mm/US 8, 60cm/24" long

&

• coiless safety pin or stitch marker

This square originally appeared in Knitter's K43.

Notes
1 See *School*, page 60, for I-cord, Make 1 (M1), and intarsia. **2** Change to circular needle when necessary.

Square
With MC, cast on 8 sts—2 on each of 4 dpn.
Rnd 1 Knit.
Rnd 2 *[K1, yo] 8 times—16 sts.
Rnd 3 Knit.
Rnd 4 *[K1, yo, k3, yo] 4 times—24 sts.
Rnd 5 Using 4 CC butterflies (1 on each needle), *[k3 MC, k1 CC, k2 MC] 4 times.
Rnd 6 [With MC, k1, yo, k2; with CC, k into front and back of next st; with MC, k2, yo] 4 times—36 sts.
Rnd 7 [With MC, k4; with CC, k1, M1, k1; with MC, k3] 4 times—40 sts.
Rnd 8 [With MC, k1, yo, k3; with CC, k3; with MC, k3, yo] 4 times—48 sts. Cont to work 2 yo incs each corner every other rnd, knitting 3 CC sts at the center of each quarter.
Tie a knot approx halfway in the CC before the end as foll: At CC location, sl 3 CC sts to dpn and work I-cord for 15 rows on the 3 I-cord sts only. Now sl the 3 sts to a coiless safety pin and tie an overhand knot in the length of cord. Place the 3 sts on left needle, k3 CC and cont. There is no need to break the yarn, just pull working yarn to back of knot after tie.
Work until square measures 11¾". With MC, k 1 rnd, p 1 rnd. With CC, k 1 rnd, p 1 rnd. With MC, k 1 rnd, p 1 rnd.
Bind off loosely.

Butterfly
Wind yarn around fingers as shown. Fasten end around center of figure 8. Butterfly feeds from the center and can substitute for a bobbin.

Gene Beugler
EUGENE, OREGON

As with most of the knitters I've talked to, I have been knitting since I was about eight years old. That seems to be a great year for a knitter to begin. When I'm not being a serious knitter or working out a fantastic new lace idea with graph paper, I can be found out in my garden either tending my vegetables, my peonies, or my rhodies.

I made this square in a fashion similar to a shawl worked from the center out so that both ends would be symmetrical. The Feather and Fan stitch is one of my favorites.

Yarn color #9489

10cm/4"
24
25
• over Chart Pat

✕

• 4.5mm/US 7, or size to
obtain gauge

&

• cable needle (cn)

This square originally
appeared in Knitter's K46.

Notes
1 See *School*, page 60, for invisible cast-on, SSK, and yo before a k and p st. **2** Square is worked from the center out towards the upper and lower edges.

Square
Cast on 52 sts using invisible cast-on. K 4 rows.
Preparation Row 1 (RS) K5, [p2, k4, p2, k9] twice, p2, k4, p2, k5.
Preparation Row 2 K5, [k2, p4, k2, p9] twice, k2, p4, k7.
Beg Chart Pat: Row 1 K5, work 17-st rep (inc'd to 25 sts) twice, work last 8 sts of chart, k5. Keeping 5 sts each side in garter st, work chart pat over center sts until 8 rows of chart have been worked 3 times, then work 2 ending rows of chart. K 9 rows. Bind off.
Remove waste yarn from cast-on edge and place 52 sts on needle, ready to work a RS row. Work 2nd half as for first half.

IN OTHER WORDS
2/2 yoLC Sl 2 to cn, hold to front, k2; yo, SSK from cn.

Chart Pat *BEGIN ON 42 STS*
Row 1 (RS) [P2, 2/2yoLC, p2, k1, yo, (k1, yo twice) 6 times, k1, yo, k1] twice, p2, 2/2yoLC, p2. **2** K2, p2, yo, p2tog, k1, [k2tog, p15 (dropping both wraps of double yo's), SSK, k1, p2, yo, p2tog, k1] twice, k1. **3** [P2, k2, yo, SSK, p17] twice, p2, k2, yo, SSK, p2. **4** K2, p2, yo, p2tog, k1, [k2tog, k13, SSK, k1, p2, yo, p2tog, k1] twice, k1. **5** [P2, k2, yo, SSK, p15] twice, p2, k2, yo, SSK, p2. **6** K2, p2, yo, p2tog, k1, [k2tog, p11, SSK, k1, p2, yo, p2tog, k1] twice, k1. **7** [P2, k2, yo, SSK, p2, k11] twice, p2, k2, yo, SSK, p2. **8** K2, p2, yo, p2tog, k1, [k2tog, p9, SSK, k1, p2, yo, p2tog, k1] twice, k1.
Rep rows 1–8 twice more.
Ending Row 1 (RS) [P2, 2/2yoLC, p2, k9] twice, p2, 2/2yoLC, p2.
Ending Row 2 Knit.

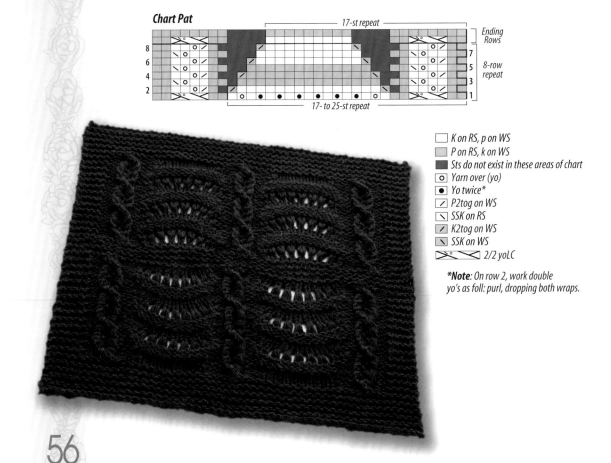

Chart Pat

17-st repeat

Ending Rows

8-row repeat

17- to 25-st repeat

☐ K on RS, p on WS
▨ P on RS, k on WS
◼ Sts do not exist in these areas of chart
⊡ Yarn over (yo)
● Yo twice*
▨ P2tog on WS
◩ SSK on RS
▨ K2tog on WS
◧ SSK on WS
✕ 2/2 yoLC

***Note:** On row 2, work double yo's as foll: purl, dropping both wraps.*

Nancy Bush

SALT LAKE CITY, UTAH

I came to knitting by way of a degree in art history—specializing in Japanese folk art—with a passion for textiles. I followed this dream to Sweden, where I studied traditional weaving. It was in the evenings, after a day at the loom, that I would try my hand at knitting. Knitting was what all the students did to relax. I found it fascinating, and as I learned more about it, I realized that there were very rich traditions connected with knitting.

My afghan square design makes use of a technique I found in an Estonian knitting book. The name for it translates as 'button stitch' and for good reason, as each little figure resembles a button. The design is formed by wrapping yarn around two stitches in a very interesting manner. I had a grand time making this square with this simple bobble-like pattern.

Yarn color #2440

10cm/4"

24

20

• *over stockinette stitch (k on RS, p on WS)*

• 4.5mm/US 7, or size to obtain gauge

This square originally appeared in Knitter's K45.

Square

Cast on 56 sts. K 5 rows, inc 4 sts evenly across on last (WS) row—60 sts. **Beg Chart Pat: Row 1** (RS) Knit. **Row 2** K3, p54, k3. Keeping first and last 3 sts in garter st, cont working chart pat over center 54 sts through chart row 64. K 6 rows, dec 4 sts evenly across first row—56 sts. Bind off.

Chart Pat *OVER 54 STS*

Rows 1 and 3 (RS) K54. **2 and all WS rows** P54. **5** K8, [BS, k16] twice, BS, k8. **7** K6, [BS, k2, BS, k12] twice, BS, k2, BS, k6. **9** K4, BS, k6, BS, k8, [BS, k2] twice, BS, k8, BS, k6, BS, k4. **11** K6, BS, k2, BS, k8, [BS, k2] 3 times, BS, k8, BS, k2, BS, k6. **13** [K8, BS] twice, [k2, BS] 4 times, k8, BS, k8. **15** K16, [BS, k2] 5 times, BS, k16. **17** K14, [BS, k2] twice, BS, k6, [BS, k2] twice, BS, k14. **19** K12, [BS, k2, BS, k6] twice, BS, k2, BS, k12. **21** K10, BS, k2, [BS, k10] twice, BS, k2, BS, k10. **23** K8, BS, k2, BS, k26, BS, k2, BS, k8. **25** K6, BS, k2, [BS, k14] twice, BS, k2, BS, k6. **27** K4, [BS, k2, BS, k14] twice, BS, k2, BS, k4. **29** [K2, BS] twice, k14, [BS, k2] twice, BS, k14, [BS, k2] twice. **31** K20, BS, k10, BS, k20. **33** [K2, BS] twice, k10, [BS, k2] 4 times, BS, k10, [BS, k2] twice. **35** Rep row 31. **37** Rep row 29. **39** Rep row 27. **41** Rep row 25. **43** Rep row 23. **45** Rep row 21. **47** Rep row 19. **49** Rep row 17. **51** Rep row 15. **53** Rep row 13. **55** Rep row 11. **57** Rep row 9. **59** Rep row 7. **61** Rep row 5. **63** Knit. **64** Purl.

Button St (BS) *OVER 2 STS*

1

Insert right needle between 2nd and 3rd sts on left needle. Wrap yarn clockwise around needle and draw a loop through.

2

Wrap yarn again clockwise around right needle and draw yarn through loop.

3

Slip 2 wrapped sts on left needle purlwise to right needle.

4

Pass 3rd st on right needle over first 2 sts.

☐ K on RS, p on WS
⊞ Button st

Chart Pat

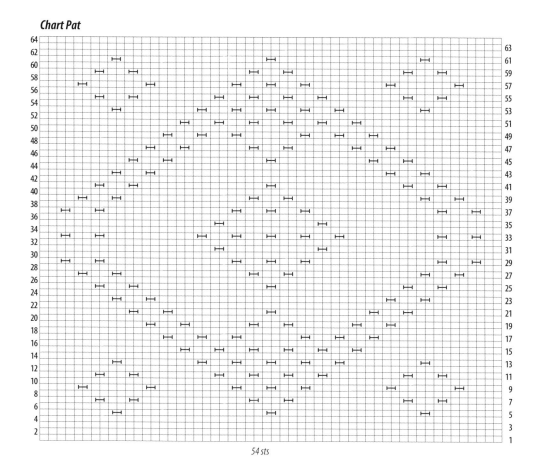

54 sts

Short rows

Uses. Each short row adds two rows of knitting across a section of the work. *Work to a certain point, turn, work back in the other direction, and repeat from* (once for one *short row*). Unless you want a hole to show at the turn, work a *wrap* as follows:

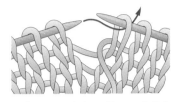

1. *Slip next stitch as if to purl. Bring yarn to right side of work and slip stitch back to left needle. Turn work, return yarn to wrong side and work to other turn point, repeat from* once.

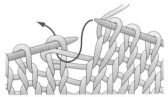

2. When you come to a wrap on the following row (or round), make it less visible by knitting or purling the wrap together with the stitch it wraps.

Cable cast-on

Uses. A cast-on that is useful when adding stitches within the work.

1. Make a slipknot on left needle.

2. Working into this knot's loop, knit a stitch and place it on left needle.

3. Insert right needle between the last 2 stitches. From this position, knit a stitch and place it on left needle. Repeat step 3 for each additional stitch.

Chain cast-on

Uses. As a *temporary cast on.*

Chain desired number with contrasting yarn. With main yarn, knit up 1 stitch in each chain, inserting needle into back loops of crochet.

Knit cast-on

1. Start with a slipknot on left needle (first cast-on stitch). Insert right needle into slipknot from front. Wrap yarn over right needle as if to knit.

2. Bring yarn through slipknot, forming a loop on right needle.
3. Insert left needle under loop and slip loop off right needle. One additional stitch cast on.

4. Insert right needle into the last stitch on left needle as if to knit. Knit a stitch and transfer it to the left needle as in Step 3. Repeat Step 4 for each additional stitch.

Knitter's SCHOOL

Invisible cast-on

Uses. As a *temporary cast on,* when access to the bottom loops is needed.

1. Knot working yarn to contrasting waste yarn. With needle in right hand, hold knot in right hand. Tension both strands in left hand; separate the strands with fingers of the left hand. Yarn over with working yarn in front of waste strand.

2. Holding waste strand taut, pivot yarns and yarn over with working yarn in back of waste strand.
3. Each yarn over forms a stitch. Alternate yarn over in front and in back of waste strand for required number of stitches. For an even number, twist working yarn around waste strand before knitting the first row.
4. Later, untie knot, remove waste strand, and arrange bottom loops on needle.

SSK

Uses. A left-slanting single decrease.

1. Slip 2 stitches separately to right needle as if to knit.

2. Knit these 2 stitches together by slipping left needle into them from left to right.

3. Knit together with right needle.

Straight-wrap cast-on

Uses. Another form of invisible cast-on, this method is used for toes of Eastern socks. The knitting proceeds in 2 directions.

1. With 2 needles held side by side and the yarn tail coming from between the 2 needles to the front, wrap the number of stitches required as indicated. There should be the same number of stitches on both needles, the yarn coming from under and between the needles to the front at the end of the wrapping.

2. With a 3rd needle, the first row is worked by knitting across top needle.

3. At the end of this needle, the work is rotated clockwise, the working yarn twisting around the tail yarn. The stitches of the 2nd needle are knit across.

S2KP2, sl 2-k1-p2sso

1. Slip 2 stitches together to right needle as if to knit.

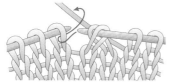

2. Knit next stitch.

3 Pass 2 slipped stitches over knit stitch and off right needle: 3 stitches become 1; the center stitch is on top.

The result is a centered double decrease.

Make 1 (M1) Knit

Uses. A single increase. (If instructions don't specify, use M1 knit, either left- or right-slanting.)

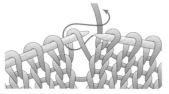

For a left-slanting increase (M1L), insert left needle from front to back under strand between last stitch knitted and first stitch on left needle. Knit, twisting strand by working into loop at back of needle.

The result is a left-slanting increase.

Or, for a right-slanting increase (M1R), insert left needle from back to front under strand between last stitch knitted and first stitch on left needle. Knit, twisting strand by working into loop at front of needle.

The result is a right-slanting increase.

SSP

Uses. A wrong side, left-slanting decrease with no twists.

1. Slip 2 stitches separately to right needle as if to knit.

2. Slip these 2 stitches back onto left needle. Insert right needle through their "back loops," into the second stitch and then the first.

3. Purl them together.

SK2P, sl 1-k2tog-psso

1. Slip 1 stitch knitwise.
2. Knit next 2 stitches together.
3. Pass the slipped stitch over the k2tog: 3 stitches become 1; the right stitch is on top.
The result is a left-slanting double decrease.

Make 1 (M1) Purl

For a left-slanting increase (M1L), insert left needle from front to back under strand between last stitch worked and first stitch on left needle. Purl, twisting strand by working into loop at back of needle from left to right.

For a right-slanting increase (M1R), work as for Make 1 Right, Knit, except purl.

Knit into front and back (kf&b)

1. Knit into front of next stitch on left needle, but do not pull the stitch off needle.
2. Take right needle to back, then knit through the back of the same stitch.

3. Pull stitch off left needle. Completed increase: 2 stitches from 1 stitch. This increase results in a purl bump after the knit stitch.

Purl into front and back (pf&b)

1. Purl into front of next stitch, but do not pull stitch off needle.
2. Take right needle to back, then through back of same stitch, from left to right...

3. ... and purl.

4. Pull stitch off left needle. Completed increase: 2 stitches from 1 stitch. This increase results in a purl bump before the stitch on the right side.

Yarn over (yo) before a K st

Bring yarn under the needle to the front, take it over the needle to the back and knit the next stitch.

Yarn over (yo) before a P st

With yarn in front of needle, bring it over the needle to the back and to the front again, purl the next stitch.

Reverse single crochet

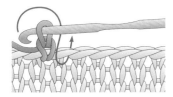

1. Reverse direction of work: work from left to right.

1a. Work a slip stitch to begin (in our example, all stitches are worked into front loop only).

1b. Enter hook into next stitch to right.

2. Bring yarn through stitch only. As soon as hook clears the stitch, flip your wrist (and the hook).

2a. There are now two loops on the hook, and the just made loop is to the front of the hook (left of the old loop).

3. Yarn over and through both loops on hook; one reverse single crochet completed.

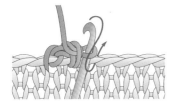

4. Continue working to right, repeating from Step 1b.

Bullion stitch

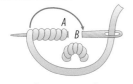

Bring needle out at A, down at B, and back out at A, then wrap yarn around tip of needle several times. Keep yarn under tension as you pull needle through wraps. Take needle to back at B to complete stitch.

French knot

I-cord

I-cord is a tiny tube of stockinette stitch, made with 2 double-pointed needles.

1. Cast on 3 (or more) stitches.

2. *Knit 3 (or more). Do not turn work. Slide stitches to right end of needle. Repeat from* for desired length. The tube forms as the yarn is pulled across the back of each row.

Twisted cord

1. Cut strands 6 times the length of cord needed. Fold in half and knot the cut ends together.

2. With knotted end in left hand and right index finger in folded end, twist clockwise until cord is tightly twisted.

3. Fold cord in half and smooth as it twists on itself; knot.

Grafting

Uses. An invisible method of joining knitting horizontally: row to row. Useful at shoulders; underarms; tips of mittens, socks, and hats. Substitute for binding off and seaming.

Stockinette graft

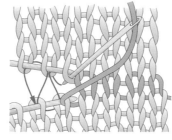

1. Arrange stitches on two needles.

2. Thread a blunt needle with matching yarn (approximately 1" per stitch).

3. Working from right to left, with right sides facing you, begin with preparatory steps 3a and 3b:

3a. Front needle: yarn through 1st loop as if to purl (from the back), leave stitch on needle.

3b. Back needle: yarn through 1st loop as if to knit (from the front), leave on.

4. Work 4a and 4b across:

4a. Front needle: through 1st stitch as if to knit, off needle: through next st as if to purl, leave on.

4b. Back needle: through 1st stitch as if to purl, off needle: through next st as if to knit, leave on.

5. Adjust tension to match rest of knitting.

Duplicate stitch

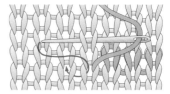

Duplicate stitch (also known as *swiss darning*) is just that: with a blunt tapestry needle threaded with a length of yarn of a con-trasting color, cover a knitted stitch with an embroidered stitch of the same shape.

abbr.

approx approximate(ly)
b in back of stitch
beg begin(ning)(s)
CC contrasting color
cn cable needle
cm centimeter(s)
cont continu(e)(ed)(es)(ing)
dec decreas(e)(ed)(es)(ing)
dpn double pointed needle(s)
foll follow(s)(ing)
g gram(s)
" inch(es)
inc increas(e)(ed)(es)(ing)
k knit(ting)(s)(ted)
LH left-hand
M1 make one
m meter(s)
MC main color
oz ounce(s)
p purl(ed)(ing)(s)
pat(s) pattern(s)
pm place marker
psso pass slipped stitch(es) over
rem remain(s)(ing)
rep repeat(s)
rev reverse(d)
RH right-hand
RS right side(s)
rnd round(s)
sc single crochet
sl slip(ped)(ping)
skp slip, knit, psso
ssk slip, slip, knit 2tog
st(s) stitch(es)
St st stockinette stitch
tbl through back of loop(s)
tog together
WS wrong side(s)
wyib with yarn in back
wyif with yarn in front
yd yard(s)
yo (2) yarn over (twice)

metrics

To convert the inches measurements used in our instructions to centimeters, simply multiply the inches by 2.5.

For example: 4" x 2.5 = 10cm

Continuations

SQUARE 7
continued from p.20

33 P1, k1, p1, k2, p2, *2/2 LPC, p5, 2/2 RPC*, p3, k2, p4, k4, S2KP2, k4, p4, k2, p3, rep between *'s once, p2, k2, p1, k1, p1. **35** K1, p1, k3, p4, *2/2 LPC, p1, 2/2 RPC*, p5, k2, p4, k3, S2KP2, k3, p4, k2, p5, rep between *'s once, p4, k3, p1, k1. **37** P1, k1, p1, k2, p6, 2/1/2 LPC, p7, k2, p2, 1-to-3 inc, p1, k2, S2KP2, k2, p1, 1-to-3 inc, p2, k2, p7, 2/1/2 RPC, p6, k2, p1, k1, p1. **39** K1, p1, k3, p6, k2, p1, k2, p7, k2, p2, M1P, k5, S2KP2, k5, M1P, p2, k2, p7, k2, p1, k2, p6, k3, p1, k1. **41** P1, k1, p1, k2, p6, k2, p1, k2, p7, k2, p3, M1P, k4, S2KP2, k4, M1P, p3, k2, p7, k2, p1, k2, p6, k2, p1, k1. **43** K1, p1, k3, p6, 2/1/2 LPC, p7, k2, p4, M1P, k3, S2KP2, k3, M1P, p4, k2, p7, 2/1/2 RPC, p6, k3, p1, k1. **45** P1, k1, p1, k2, p4, 2/2 RPC, p1, 2/2 LPC, p5, k2, p5, M1P, k2, S2KP2, k2, M1P, p5, k2, p5, 2/2 RPC, p1, 2/2 LPC, p4, k2, p1, k1, p1. **47** K1, p1, k3, p2, *2/2 RPC, p2, 1-to-5 inc, p2, 2/2 LPC*, p3, k2, p6, k1, S2KP2, k1, p6, k2, p3, rep between *'s once, p2, k3, p1, k1. **49** P1, k1, p1, k2, *2/2 RPC, p4, k5, p4, 2/2 LPC*, p1, k2, p6, S2KP2, p6, k2, p1, rep between *'s once, k2, p1, k1, p1. **50** K1, p1, k1, p4, k17, p2, k1, p2, k6, p1, k6, p2, k1, p2, k17, p4, k1, p1, k1. **51** K1, p1, k1, 2/2 PKLC, p6, Acorn Cap St, p6, 2/1/2 LPC, p6, k1, p6, 2/1/2 RPC, p6, Acorn Cap St, p6, 2/2 KPRC, k1, p1, k1. **52** [P1, k1] twice, p3, *k6, p2tog, p1, SSP, k6*, p2, k1, p2, k6, p1, k6, p2, k1, p2, rep between *'s once, p3, [k1, p1] twice. **53** [P1, k1] twice, p1, 2/2 KPLC, p4, S2KP2, p4, 2/2 RPC, p1, 2/2 LPC, p9, 2/2 RPC, p1, 2/2 LPC, p4, S2KP2, p4, 2/2 PKRC, p1, [k1, p1] twice. **55** [K1, p1] 3 times, k1, 2/2 PKLC, *p5, 2/2 RPC, p2, 1-to-5 inc, p2, 2/2 LPC*, rep between *'s once, p5, 2/2 KPRC, k1, [p1, k1] 3 times. **57** [P1, k1] 4 times, p1, 2/2 KPLC, *p1, 2/2 RPC, p4, k5, p4, 2/2 LPC*, rep between *'s once, p1, 2/2 PKRC, p1, [k1, p1] 4 times. **58** [K1, p1] 6 times, p1, k1, p2, k17, p2, k1, p2, k17, [p2, k1] twice, [p1, k1] 5 times. **59** [K1, p1] 5 times, k1, 2/1/2 LPC, [p6, Acorn Cap St, p6, 2/1/2 RPC] twice, k1, [p1, k1] 5 times. **60** [P1, k1] 7 times, p2, *k6, p2tog, p1, SSP, k6*, p5, rep between *'s once, p2, [k1, p1] 7 times. **61** [P1, k1] 7 times, 2/2 PKLC, p4, S2KP2, p4, 2/2 RC, k1, 2/2 LC, p4, S2KP2, p4, 2/2 KPRC, [k1, p1] 7 times. **63** [K1, p1] 8 times, 2/2 KPLC, p5, 2/2 RC, k5, 2/2 LC, p5, 2/2 PKRC, [p1, k1] 8 times. **65** [P1, k1] 9 times, 2/2 PKLC, p1, 2/2 RC, k9, 2/2 LC, p1, 2/2 KPRC, [k1, p1] 9 times. **67** [K1, p1] 10 times, 2/1/2 LPC, k13, 2/1/2 RPC, [p1, k1] 10 times. **68** [P1, k1] 11 times, p19, [k1, p1] 11 times. **69** [P1, k1] 11 times, p1, 2/2 KPLC, k9, 2/2 PKRC, [p1, k1] 11 times. **71** [K1, p1] 12 times, k1, 2/2 PKLC, k5, 2/2 KPRC, k1, [p1, k1] 12 times. **73** [P1, k1] 13 times, p1, 2/2 KPLC, k1, 2/2 PKRC, p1, [k1, p1] 13 times. **75** [K1, p1] 14 times, k1, 2/1/2 RPC, k1, [p1, k1] 14 times. **77** [P1, k1] 15 times, k1, p1, k1, [k1, p1] 15 times. **79** Rep row 75. **80** [P1, k1] 14 times, p3, k1, p3, [k1, p1] 14 times.

SQUARE 12
continued from p.30

Chart pats

Chart A Rows 1, 3, 5 (WS) Sl 1, k16. **2, 4** Sl 1, p15, SSK. **6** Sl 1, p7, k1, p7, SSK. **7 and all foll WS rows** Sl 1, k the knits and p the purls. **8** Sl 1, p5, [k1, p1] twice, k1, p5, SSK. **10, 12, 14, 16** Sl 1, p3, [k1, p1] 4 times, k1, p3, SSK. **18** Sl 1, p3, 3/6 Rib RC, p3, SSK. **20** Rep row 10. **22** Sl 1, p3, MB, [p1, k1] 3 times, p1, MB, p3, SSK. **24** Sl 1, p5, MB, p1, k1, p1, MB, p5, SSK. **26** Sl 1, p7, MB, p7, SSK. **28, 30, 32, 34** Rep row 2.

Chart B Row 1 (RS) Sl 1, [k1, p1] 7 times, k2. **2** Sl 1, p2, [k1, p1] 3 times, k2, p2, k1, p1, k1, p2tog. **3** Sl 1, k1, p1, k3, p3, [k1, p1] twice, k4. **4** Sl 1, p4, k1, p1, k4, p4, k1, p2tog. **5** Sl 1, k5, p5, k6. **6** Sl 1, p5, k5, p5, p2tog. **7** Sl 1, k4, p1, k1, p4, k4, p1, k1. **8** Sl 1, p1, k1, p3, k3, [p1, k1] twice, p3, p2tog. **9** Sl 1, k2, [p1, k1] 3 times, p2, k2, [p1, k1] twice. **10** Sl 1, [p1, k1] 7 times, p1, p2tog. **11** Sl 1, [p1, k1] 8 times. **12** Sl 1, p1, k1, p1, k2, p2, [k1, p1] 3 times, k2, p2tog. **13** Sl 1, p3, [k1, p1] twice, k3, p3, k1, p1, k1. **14** Sl 1, p1, k4, p4, k1, p1, k4, p2tog. **15** Sl 1, p5, k5, p5, k1. **16** Sl 1, k5, p5, k5, p2tog. **17** Sl 1, k1, p4, k4, p1, k1, p4, k1. **18** Sl 1, k3, [p1, k1] twice, p3, k3, p1, k1, p2tog. **19** Sl 1, k1, p1, k1, p2, k2, [p1, k1] 3 times, p2, k1. **20** Sl 1, [k1, p1] 7 times, k1, p2tog. **21–34** Rep rows 1–14.

Chart C Row 1 (RS) Sl 1, p3, k9, p3, k1. **2** Sl 1, k3, p9, k3, p2tog. **3** Sl 1, p3, 1/3 LC, k1, 1/3 RC, p3, k1. **4** Sl 1, k3, p9, k3, p2tog. **5–32** Rep rows 1–4. **33–34** Rep rows 1–2.

Chart D: Rows 1, 3 (WS) Sl 1, k15, p1. **2** Sl 1, p15, SSK. **4, 6** Sl 1, p14, k1, SSK. **5, 7** Sl 1, p1, k14, p1. **8** Sl 1, p12, 1/2 RPC, SSK. **9** Sl 1, k2, p1, k12, p1. **10** Sl 1, p10, 1/2 Rib RC, p2, SSK. **11**: Sl 1, k2, p1, k1, p1, k10, p1. **12** Sl 1, p8, 1/2 RPC, p1, k1, p2, SSK. **13** Sl 1, k2, p1, k3, p1, k8, p1. **14** Sl 1, p6, 1/2 Rib RC, p1, 1/2 RPC, p2, SSK. **15** Sl 1, k4, [p1, k1] twice, p1, k6, p1. **16** Sl 1, p4, 1/2 RPC, p1, k1, p1, 1-to-5-inc, p4, SSK—21 sts. **17** Sl 1, k4, p5, k1, p1, k3, p1, k4, p1. **18** Sl 1, p4, k1, p1, 1/2 RPC, p1, k5, p4, SSK. **19** Sl 1, k4, p5, k3, p1, k1, p1, k4, p1. **20** Sl 1, p4, k1, p1, 1-to-5 inc, p3, 5-to-3 dec, p4, SSK—23 sts. **21** Sl 1, k4, p3, k3, p5, k1, p1, k4, p1. **22** Sl 1, p2, 1/2 RPC, p1, k5, p3, S2KP2, p4, SSK—21 sts. **23** Sl 1, k8, p5, k3, p1, k2, p1. **24** Sl 1, p2, 1-to-5 inc, p3, 5-to-3 dec, p8, SSK—23 sts. **25** Sl 1, k8, p3, k3, p5, k2, p1. **26** Sl 1, p2, k5, p3, S2KP2, p8, SSK—21 sts. **27** Sl 1, k12, p5, k2, p1. **28** Sl 1, p2, 5-to-3 dec, p12, SSK—19 sts. **29** Sl 1, k12, p3, k2, p1. **30** Sl 1, p2, S2KP2, p12, SSK—17 sts. **31, 33** Sl 1, k15, p1. **32, 34** Sl 1, p15, SSK.

SQUARE 21
continued from p.50

44 P3, k3, p2, k3, p1, k5, p1, k7, p8, k5, p3, k4, [p1, k2] twice, p1. **45** K1, p2, 1/1 LPC, 1/1 RPC, p3, 1/1 RPC, 2/1LPC, p4, k1, p7, k3, yo, SSK, k3, p2, MB, p2, k12. **46** P1, k10, p1, k2, sl 1, k2, p8, k7, p1, k4, p2, k2, p1, k4, p2, k3, p1. **47** K1, p3, 2/1 LPC, p2, 1/1 RPC, p2, 2/1LPC, p3, k1, p7, k1, k2tog, yo, k1, yo, SSK, k2, p5, k12. **48** [P1, k1] 5 times, p2, k5, p8, k7, p1, k3, p2, k4, p1, k2, p2, k4, p1. **49** K1, p4, 2/1 LPC, 1/1 RPC, p3, 1/1 RPC, 1/1 LPC, p2, k1, p7, k2tog, yo, k3, yo, SSK, k1, p5, [k1, p1] 5 times, k2. **50** [P1, k1] 5 times, p2, k5, p8, k7, p1, [k2, p1] twice, k4, p3, k5, p1. **51** K1, p5, 3/1LPC, p2, 1/1 RPC, p2, 1/1 LPC, p1, k1, p7, k2, yo, SK2P, yo, k3, p5, [k1, p1] 5 times, k2. **52** [P1, k1] 5 times, p2, k5, p8, k7, [p1, k1] twice, k3, p1, k2, p3, k6, p1. **53** K1, p6, 3/1 LPC, 1/1 RPC, p3, 1/1 RPC, p1, k1, p7, k3, yo, SSK, k3, p2, MB, p2, [k1, p1] 5 times, k2. **54** [P1, k1] 5 times, p2, k2, sl 1, k2, p8, k7, p1, k2, p1, k4, p4, k7, p1. **55** K1, p4, p2tog, k1, 4/1LIC, p2, 1/1 RPC, p2, k4, yo, SSK, k2, p7, k1, p5, [k1, p1] 5 times, k2. **56** [P1, k1] 5 times, p2, k5, p1, k7, p8, k3, p1, k2, p7, k5, p1. **57** K1, p3, p2tog, k3, 4/1LIC, 1/1 RPC, p3, k2, k2tog, yo, k1, yo, SSK, k1, p7, k1, p5, k12. **58** P1, k10, p1, k5, p1, k7, p8, k4, p10, k4, p1. **59** K1, p2, p2tog, k5, M2P, k5, p2tog, p2, k1, k2tog, yo, k3, yo, SSK, p7, k1, p5, k12. **60** P5, k1, p4, k1, p1, k5, p1, k7, p8, k3, p5, k2, p5, k3, p1. **61** K1, p3, k5, p2, k5, p3, k3, yo, SK2P, yo, k2, p7, k1, p2, MB, p2, k1, [p2, k3] twice, k1. **62** P3, k3, p2, k3, p1, k2, p1, k7, p8, k2, [p2tog, p4] twice, p2tog, k2, p1. **63** K20, yo, SSK, k2, p7, k1, p5, [k1, p4] twice, k2. **64** P1, k10, p1, k5, p1, k7, p8, k16. **65** K32, p5, k12. **66** P1, k10, p1, k5, p1, k1, kf&b, [p1, k6] 4 times, p1. **67** K1, [p5, 1/1RC] 4 times, p3, k1, p5, k12. **68** P5, k1, p4, k1, p1, k5, p1, k3, [p2, k5] 4 times, p1. **69** K1, [p3, k1, 1/1RC, k1] 4 times, p3, k1, p2, MB, p2, k1, [p2, k3] twice, k1. **70** P3, k3, p2, k3, p1, k2, sl 1, k2, p1, [k3, p4] 4 times, k3, p1. **71** K1, [p3, (k1, M1) twice, k2] 4 times, p3, k1, p5, k1, [p4, k1] twice, k1. **72** P1, k10, p1, k5, p1, [k3, p6] 4 times, k3, p1. **73** K1, [p3, k2, M1, k1, M1, k3] 4 times, p3, k1, p5, k12. **74** P1, k10, p1, k5, p1, [k3, p8] 4 times, k3, p1. **75** K1, [p3, SSK, k3, k2tog, k1] 4 times, p3, k1, p5, k12. **76** P5, k1, p4, k1, p1, k5, p1, [k3, p6] 4 times, k3, p1. **77** K1, [p3, SSK, k1, k2tog, M1P, k1] 4 times, p3, k1, p2, MB, p2, k1, p2, k3, p2, k4. **78** P3, k3, p2, k3, p1, k2, sl 1, k2, p1, [k3, p1, k1, p3] 4 times, k3, p1. **79** K1, [p3, SK2P, M1P, p1, k1] 3 times, p3, SK2P, M1P, p1, SSK, p2, k1, p5, [k1, p4] twice, k2. **80** P1, k10, p1, k5, p1, k2, [p1, k6] 4 times, p1.

Watch our online video and you'll fall in love with each of these 25 glorious squares—even before you pick up your needles.

Come get square with us at

knittinguniverse.com/GETSQUARE